Making Solo Pe

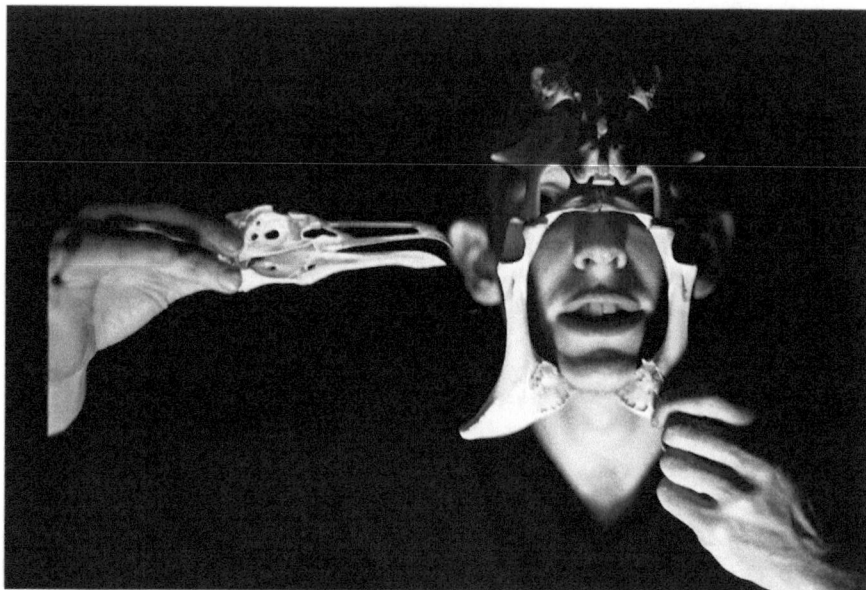

Deaf Birds, Late Snow (1978) ©Steve Allison

Misri Dey

Making Solo Performance

Six Practitioner Interviews

macmillan
education

palgrave

First published 2018 by
PALGRAVE

Palgrave in the UK is an imprint of Macmillan Publishers Limited, registered in England, company number 785998, of 4 Crinan Street, London N1 9XW.

Palgrave® and Macmillan® are registered trademarks in the United States, the United Kingdom, Europe and other countries.

ISBN 978–1–137–60325–8 paperback
ISBN 978–1–137–60326–5 hardback

This book is printed on paper suitable for recycling and made from fully managed and sustained forest sources. Logging, pulping and manufacturing processes are expected to conform to the environmental regulations of the country of origin.

A catalogue record for this book is available from the British Library.

A catalog record for this book is available from the Library of Congress.

For Dr. Andrea Hunt (Andy); constant, loving, attacks life and always inspiring.

Table of Contents

List of Images

Acknowledgements

Thank you – To the solo practitioners: Bobby Baker, Nigel Charnock, Tim Etchells, Wendy Houstoun, Bryony Kimmings, and Mike Pearson, for your time, words and then more time spent on computers getting edits and pictures to me. Thank you to photographers Hugo Glendinning, Christa Holke, Chris Nashe, Andrew Whittuck, Steve Allison, Graham Chance Clayton, Nick Mercer and Russell Basford, for their pictures and generosity. To my partner and son, for putting up with me: Louis Purver and Leo Dey. To my family: Andy, Valentina, Chiara, David, Tom and Paula, for just being alive and around. To Chris Crickmay, for constant feedback and editing help, and to Jennie Crickmay, for food and laughter. Thank you to my colleagues, from the earlier radical, beautiful small place of learning, Dartington College of Arts, and especially John Hall and David Williams, who supported my original PhD research that these interviews fed into. Also to past and current Falmouth University colleagues, in particular Danielle, Klaus, Aiden, Gregg, Richard, Joan, Aga, Mark and Terrie, who work their socks off, and John Freeman who said 'just do it' at the right time. I also thank my students, for having roaring imaginations. From the Solo Contemporary Performance Forum, I thank Ria Hartley, solo artist and activist, and Hannah Sullivan, solo artist and producer, for their brilliant minds, work and general excellence. Finally, thank you to Nicola Cattini and Clarissa Sutherland at Palgrave, for initially supporting this book into publication.

Introduction

Imagine reading a performance flyer:

'A Lecture upon Heads', including: 'Humorous Oration in Praise of the Law, Nobody's, Somebody's, Anybody's and Everybody's...Family of Nobody's'.[1]

You decide to watch the show. The performer satirises the law and current politics and challenges colonising narratives dressed up as heroisms. One 'Head' is that of Alexander the Great, whose 'greatness' is sharply examined and critiqued. This solo performance could easily be mistaken for contemporary political stand-up comedy, akin to Steward Lee or Bridget Christie. In fact, it dates from 1765, and, in its own right, brought the monologue as art form to public attention. This work by George Alexander Stevens was hugely popular and was performed and re-performed by others more than 1,000 times to crowded salons in eighteenth-century London and Europe. Yet initially, Stevens, as a solo artist, could not legally perform anywhere.[2] Artists are often expected to be trangressive, and solo artists in particular have a reputation for being strange, anti-social, illegal creatures. A multitude of marvellous bodies populated Renaissance fayres and travelling circuses, challenging the boundaries of what it meant to be man, woman, human, beast. More recently, graffiti artists, like early Banksy, moved art canvases out from galleries onto the streets and subways; the infamous NEA (National Endowment for the Arts) four – Karen Finlay, Holly Hughes, Tim Miller and John Fleck – all had their proposed government art awards vetoed due to the subject matter of their work[3]; in 1974, Philippe Petit performed a high-wire dance for an hour between the twin towers of the World Trade Center, before being arrested and cautioned. Stevens was an early example of one such maverick outlaw – literally performing without licence to audiences who clearly enjoyed the subterfuge and were alive to its unauthorised nature.

Solo

The term 'solo', when used as an adjective, offers a proposition of oneness, of being alone, unaccompanied or unassisted. It defines a well-known way of working in all the arts, where it forms either part of a group practice – scriptwriter, choreographer, composer – or is a practice in itself, as with a painter, sculptor, musician, photographer or writer.

This sense of 'as if' oneness, of aloneness yet being 'with' others carried on into the later development of the word 'soloist' in the mid-nineteenth century. The soloist plays a singular line of music amidst an orchestra, as in a concerto. The performing soloist as musician is separated from the orchestra, even as it accompanies her or him. Again, the nature of the 'solo' state of being here does not in fact mean being solitary, but rather being literally 'outstanding', physically separated from the other musicians and playing a usually virtuosic, individual line of music.

Solitary practices also have historical legacies in religion, philosophy, coming-of-age rituals and aviation. The solo aviator crosses the Atlantic for the first time, delivering the night mail; the solo dancer or violinist is framed by light, demonstrating perfect technique; and the philosopher walks and thinks, alone. Religion offers us the practice of 'eremitage', choosing to be a hermit, anchorite or (lit) 'desert dweller', isolated in order to inspire 'face to face' experience with the divine.[4] Global rites of coming of age include being thrust alone into the wilderness, to do battle with nature and forces unknown.

Defining Solo and the Focus of this Book

I am working with a definition of 'solo' in a making and performing context as being where one person is responsible for creating and holding the vision of a piece of work, from idea to performance, although others may be involved in its making. It is important here to add that an overly simplistic view of the solo performer as singular, working entirely alone and in isolation, is not the theme of this book, or a true reflection of practice. The practitioners included here make and perform solo and balance at least three roles: those of deviser, director and performer. It will also emerge in the interviews that the artists concerned firstly make regular use of others in their working processes, and secondly, collaborate 'with' their audiences in a way that makes them far from alone.

Whilst there is clearly a wide variety of solo theatre and performance forms, operating across both popular and experimental work and across arts disciplines, this book specifically focuses on the 'postdramatic' end of the spectrum of solo theatre practice – work that, among other things, goes beyond the primacy of a script.

'Further', the focus of this book is on solo *making* processes: what they are, how they are carried out and what they can entail. With the advent of popular media, YouTube, Vimeo and webcasts of live events, we have unprecedented access to versions of live theatre work. But we seldom have access to how that work is made – to the rehearsal space, which can be in a studio or at home, and the many detailed processes that go into creating a production. What often fails to reach audiences is the labour, expertise and craft involved in making. What is at stake is an invisibility and potential lack of valuing of these processes. This has consequences for funding and generally for the status of the work. However, talking about how one makes something is hard, and, at times, perhaps impossible – to rationalise what can sometimes be intuitive or non-verbal. This gap between doing something and speaking about doing something can, however, be acknowledged, without giving up on the attempt to verbalise and share knowledge. Practitioners themselves have multiple insights to contribute and can offer one important, informed version of what they do. These kinds of personal accounts are notable by their absence in the public arenas – for example in academic publishing or newspaper critical columns.

As an arts educator, I teach acting and theatre making. Questions of value, like 'What is good work and how do you make it?' are critical in the academy. Susan Melrose, writing on performance-making processes, asks pertinent questions about expertise in the arts, like what is it and how do we get it? What does it look like?[5] Such questions need explicit answers, as we charge students to learn theatre expertise and assess them on what they have learned. This book offers numerous examples of expertise relevant to the above questions.

In a sense, our wider culture idolises the soloist. We have never before been so engaged with the cult of celebrity, the 'stars' who may be virtuosic or simply notorious. The twenty-first century viciously fosters individualism, in ever-expanding global capitalist economies, and yet people have never been so homogenised. There is pressure to both conform and also be 'unique', as individuals and even as a nation. In the UK, in a post-Brexit climate, we are engaged in a geopolitical wrestling match between the illusion of an individual nation state and deep knowing of the ultimate power of the collective. It seems a useful skill, at present, to be able to negotiate individual ambition, desire, obsession and interest with group intelligence, expertise and strengths.

In a small way, these conversations about solo making contribute ideas to this debate. The practitioners interviewed make work they care about. They have something to individually say, and do, in performance. They also model ways of working which embrace collaboration and perform collages of multiple voices and viewpoints. The North American writer Richard Sennett, who has written on expert crafting and collaboration, identifies contemporary society as offering two brutal and simple edicts: 'us against them' coupled with 'you are on your own' (2012: 280). These solo practitioners speak of enjoying creative spaces where they can be deeply on their own, precisely because they are also severally connected with other practitioners, makers, producers and audiences – alone with others.

A Very Brief History of Solo Performance

The term 'solo' means something different in theatre, dance and arts practices. My focus of discussion here is on solo drama, theatre and performance practices, which inevitably have a complex, intertwined history and of which I offer here a brief suggestion of the rich variety. One can begin in the oration and monologues of Greek address and the tales of minstrels, fools and medieval travelling artists, messages directed to the populace as well as their rulers. Subversion was and is written into fooling, an early example of satire and humour used to couch often serious messages of social dissent and critique. For wider public consumption, fayres and circuses, like Bartholomew Fayre of seventeenth- and eighteenth-century England, provided arenas for the parade of solo entertainment: freaks, special acts, acrobats, magicians and fortune tellers who created intimate one-to-one performances, provoking and challenging their audiences with tricks and transformations. The monologue as oratory or lecture continued and grew in popularity during the Restoration in the UK with satirists like Stevens and Foote performing the *Lecture upon Heads* (1765) or *The Diversions of the Morning* (1747). These specific examples of early solo performance from the eighteenth century lay some foundations for characteristics and ideas about it, which later recurred. These include solo having an ambiguous status, 'illegitimate' yet very popular, crossing social activity boundaries, as both artistic performance and social event. Later on, this was further developed in traditions of Victorian old time music hall in the early nineteenth century and in comedy, stand-up and cabaret. It aimed to be of widespread appeal, frequently satirical and self-reflexive, with both performers and audiences holding a beer in the hand.

The monologue gained traction as drama in the 'monopolylogue', where one person plays several roles, like Charles Matthews's early three-act multi-character farce *At Homes* (1818) and William Gillette's Sherlock Holmes (1899). Moving into the next century, other popular and equally enduring solo work included further variations on the monologue form in dramatic biographies of famous individuals' lives, for example Hal Holbrook's *Mark Twain Tonight!* (1954), numerous performances about Gertrude Stein (Pat Carroll, 1970), *The Belle of Amherst* and *Bronte* (Julie Harris, 1976). This kind of portrayal emphasised the skill of the actor, in playing a character other than themselves. A related 'showcase' model is the monodrama written for a particular individual performer. Well-known examples include Jean Cocteau writing *Le Bel Indifférent* for Edith Piaf, first performed in 1940, and Samuel Beckett writing *Krapp's Last Tape* in 1957 for Patrick Magee,

Marisa Fabbri in *The Bacchae* (1976), and more recently Simon Callow in Peter Ackroyd's *The Mystery of Charles Dickens* (2012). This work again contributes to the association of solo work with performing virtuosity: the performer inhabits and switches between different characters, using spoken word, gesture, movement, and costume to represent the dramatic narrative.

A later, very different kind of monopolylogue work moving into post-dramatic terrain is the solo verbatim theatre of Anna Deveare Smith. In it, she engages with real people and issues, most famously in situations of political or racial conflict. Her most well-known solo works include *Fires in the Mirror* (1991) and *Twilight, Los Angeles* (1992). However, Deveare Smith makes no attempt to use theatrical signifiers such as costume or light or mise-en-scène to create an illusion of 'being' these people: she works solely with voice, gesture and their edited narratives, to 'walk in their words'.[6] She performs a more fluid, inter-subjectivity: the multi-vocal montage of 'American' voices into which her own is mixed.

Solo performance is also prevalent in theatre forms that do not rely on dramatic narrative as the primary organising structure. Work in the *Commedia dell'arte* tradition, ranging from Dario Fo's religious satire *Mistero Buffo (1988)* with to the inclusion of vaudeville in Geoff Hoyle's *The Fool Show* (1988) and Stephen Wade's *Banjo Dancing* (1979), all prioritise strong performer presences rather than character and situations rather than plot structure and allow improvisation into the performance.

Comedy has a long tradition of solo working, traditionally occurring in a sociable environment. The 'joke' as a primary motif introduces the extreme dynamic within which much solo comedy performance operates, starkly revealing both performer skill and ever-present potential failure. In its live mode, it also relies strongly on an intimate connection with the audience, who are near and who can engage in live, direct and often confrontational address. Bryony Kimmings comes from this tradition of club stand-up, and this is evident in her very close tracking of the audience. Earlier traditions of magic and cabaret, started in Paris in 1881, also centralised the solo performer, and while cabaret's heyday was in the early part of the twentieth century, one can connect to it later developments of a particular strand of performance art. In New York in the 1980s and 1990s, and fast-made, trashy performance art experimented with new solo forms and invited in new audiences. Wendy Houstoun similarly locates London both in the 1980s and in 2010 as a time where such multi-disciplinary solo experimentation also flourished. She speaks of small London pub venues like the Rosemary Branch (Islington), the Hemingford Arms (Islington) or the Oxford Arms (Camden) and later Greenwich Town Hall, home of Friday Night Cabaret, as important small venues where diverse short pieces of solo material could be shown.

Moving across disciplines, visual art practices in the 1930s and the art of the Dadaists and Surrealists moved art work out of formal galleries, which placed specific value on it in relation to a commercial market, and presented instead in temporary exhibition spaces[7]. They went onto the city streets with the ambulatory work of the Situationists and subsequent site-specific graffiti and public art. This laid the groundwork for the solo site-specific work of Pearson, Houstoun and Baker.

Developing out of fine art in the USA in the 1960s, with parallels in Europe in 'action art', pursued by Beuys and others, performance art was and is typically performed solo (even though, interestingly, its immediate predecessor, the 'Happenings' of the 1950s, were typically group events). Performance art developed in the UK ten years after its USA counterpart and arose out of different initial contexts.[8] Historical performance art practices brought live performance into gallery settings and out to other sites. It offered solo autobiographical monologues and task-based processes of working, emphasising endurance over time, or the carrying out of a single concept rather than a series of actions as in theatre. Bobby Baker helped create these traditions.

My Solo Practice

For my own part, this work grew from my previous engagement in solo performance practice. I started making solo work in 2003, exploring my mixed ethnicity, and a number of questions came up in doing this, which I then put to other solo makers. These included how to have multiple voices in a solo, the different kinds of collaboration possible within solo working, how to work with important contemporary issues which concerned me (ethnic discrimination, geopolitics, population control, adoption) without seeming like a mad preacher and completely losing my audience, the art of folding in humour and lightness to weightier topics. Added to this, I also questioned how to work beyond autobiography and a number of other issues. I wondered how other people dealt with these, behind the necessarily closed doors of studio practice, particularly those who had been doing it for a long time. In 2004, in a lab with the Solo Contemporary Performance Forum, it became evident that these and other issues were shared by most other solo practitioners. Following that experience, I sought a more intensive way to address the questions. I undertook a series of extended interviews with six solo performance makers whose work I admired, which now form the basis of this book. I was fortunate enough to be given this very generous and privileged access to their thinking and reflection.

The Practitioners

The practitioners included in this book are Bryony Kimmings, Bobby Baker, Tim Etchells, Mike Pearson, Wendy Houstoun and Nigel Charnock. I chose solo practitioners with backgrounds in either theatre, Live Art or dance, who work within a 'theatre event' idea of performance,[9] namely they all priortise experiment, and consciously use and abuse theatre conventions, devices and frames.

Bryony Kimmings performs funny, vibrant, trashy, no-holds-barred solo performance, addressing her audience directly: 'Hello My name is Bryony...', and then launching into an aural and visual feast of spoken autobiographical monologues, songs and dances, with numerous objects. She is provocatively autobiographical, as in her infamous first solo *Sex Idiot* (2010), where she challenges notions of sex and the body as individualised or privatised by inviting the audience to cut off and contribute some of their pubic hair, which she gathers and makes into a moustache. She works as a theatre activist, speaking about current uncomfortable social and health issues such as cancer, sexual diseases, mental health, the policing of children's imaginations and child poverty. She manages this subject matter with a detailed light touch and a performed persona, which she allows to be both simultaneously likeable and annoying, funny and serious, tough and vulnerable. This is a ludicrously honest approach, allowing diverse and contradictory perspectives into the work, and reflects the true complexity of her subject matter.

Tim Etchells is a highly experienced writer, director and performer, known for his work with the theatre collective Forced Entertainment but also perhaps less known for his solo work, which he has engaged in simultaneously for many years. This includes theatre and video performance, books, and neon sign writing, installation and gallery exhibitions. He has worked for years around the question of what theatre needs or does not need, to exist, function and entertain. He also explores what artwork can do on a page, stage, and gallery space or in digital form. He has an acute dramaturgical and compositional sensibility – an expertise in standing back, to view a theatre piece as an 'economy' or working system which needs fine tuning, both in rehearsal and in performance. He is a quiet maverick with a performance persona that disarms through being casual and seemingly everyday, and yet beneath this lies a master orchestrator, composing intricate work with the random materials he has been sent by others. The result is often complex and dark and requires work from the viewer, whom he coaxes and deceives into thinking all is safe and easy. In his own working process, he emphasises the need for reflective time and solitary contemplation. Solo working fits him well, being perhaps a familiar state for a person who does a lot of writing as part of his practice.

Wendy Houstoun's solo work and the ways she speaks about it reveal clearly her strong physical and dance expertise. She prioritises physicality, her body and its intelligent knowing. Her early foundational work with the dance theatre company DV8 and Ludus Dance clearly informs this, as does her creation of subsequent numerous solos. She offers up what she refers to as personal manifestos in performance form. She uses dance, spoken word and film, to observe and transpose the state of the world into her work. Her performance persona is often contradictory; low-key, oblique, pedestrian and yet clearly propelled by an underlying anger and critique. She is a master at working with energetic states, frequently changing the dynamic of the work, disarming an audience who may expect to be told verbally but who are shown, physically, instead.

Laughter formed the baseline of Bobby Baker's interviews. Her approach to speaking and to making work shares irreverence and a furious exuberance that is also present in conversation with her. And she certainly is a conversationalist – her interview is packed full of examples of how she uses discussion to advance her making processes. Baker has been making performance work for more than forty years, highlighting in part how our contemporary image of a woman still remains buried under inaccurate notions of the so-called domestic realm: of (grand) motherhood, shopping, housework, mental health and family. As you might expect of a person coming from visual art, her work often begins with objects and specific locations, which she orchestrates with great dexterity, weaving them around her autobiographical narratives. She populates her work with many Bobby Bakers – from mother to cabaret dancer to grandmother to artist to wife to social activist to mental health patient, while always playing with the tone and aim of what she does, to challenge, disconcert, woo, engage and tickle her audience. She works with enormous detail, precision and patience to create works that look chaotic, temporary and messy. A thrilling mess; of objects, music, words, songs – all spilling out over tablecloths and baths, church floors and fields. Baker also speaks freely about intuitive working, which she mixes into her precisely planned work, to great effect.

Mike Pearson is most often known for his large-scale, spectacular site work such as, with Cardiff Laboratory Theatre and Brith Goff in the 1970s and 1980s. But he has also made recurrent, small-scale solo work throughout his long career. His are the aesthetics of extremity, challenging himself to learn and explore. He 'excavates' places, draws out their histories and stories and re-performs these to the communities who live there. His solo work has drawn out of him the ability to perform long monologues, akin to Greek tragedies, where he does not leave the stage and speaks continually. The opposite end of this is his creation of audio walks where he himself is absent and it is instead the audience who 'perform' the work, to explore place and story. He has also been an academic for the past twenty years and has written three books on performance, site and making, which illustrate his dramaturgical and precise compositional approach, also clearly manifest in the interviews.

Nigel Charnock died in 2012, subsequent to these interviews. He could be affectionately described as an 'exquisite irritant', in life, interview and performance. From his early work with DV8, his performances were provocative, high energy, vibrant and loud. His choreographic approach was relentlessly physical, precise and clear, informed by his dance training and continued pursuit of both technical and improvisatory excellence. He embraced contradiction, tension, argument and passion, alternately praising and insulting his audiences. His solo work was unashamedly autobiographical, giving form to his concerns about huge subject areas such as life, relationships, death, men and women. He performed high-status personae – he was not one for low-key humility. You got what you saw and as an audience you had to be involved. He went out to his audiences, sweated on them, and threw real sweets and metaphorical grenades, simultaneously. He was passionate about the state of the world and highly critical of our dubious place within it, furious at the English's contempt for performance, but always insistent that he enjoyed his work and working.

As is evident, these interviewees come from different disciplines within performance. Between them, they create a wide range of solo work as site-specific theatre, audio walks, autobiographical monologues, stand-up, physical theatre, cabaret, dance-theatre, live and performance art, durational events and performance lectures. What they share is a clear connection to what is now often termed 'postdramatic' performance practices.[10] They do not work with representing a scripted, dramatic narrative but instead experiment with multiple media to explore thematic interests and events arising out of the live theatre situation and their relationship with their audience. Theatre labours under the strong expectation of telling a story, and all theatrical elements are employed to serve this telling. Postdramatic work liberates space, time, writing, light, sound and also the actor and the audience from serving the story and instead allows them to become the story itself. Performance becomes an event, not a tale told. Solo postdramatic work, made by all these interviewees, works in the above ways. Solo performance intensifies the postdramatic audience–performer relationship. There is one axis of communication, between these two central protagonists – the audience and the performer.

Some Similarities and Differences

What emerges from this book is a rich and varied set of articulations about how solo performances can be made, with some shared ways of working evident as well as multiple differences. Differences inevitably arise in the interview discussions themselves – different topics and preoccupations emerge as between one interviewee and another, not to mention the different ways of speaking about work. In addition, the interviews reveal different motivations for working, different methods of making work and different compositional styles.

Shared meeting points abound, in different configurations. So Pearson and Etchells shared a strong overarching compositional perspective on the work even before it was made, Etchells speaking about it as an 'economy' or game, Pearson as dramaturgy, a timeline with blanks to be filled in. Baker and Kimmings share a prioritisation of their use of objects to bounce off ideas and narratives, 'step by step' with Baker and a strong use of humour wrapped around the issues they are passionate to discuss. Houstoun and Charnock prioritise physical improvising, thirty seconds of making choreographic material a day, 'just getting in there and doing it,' as ways they gather material.

The performance persona created by these different practitioners revealed elasticity in the kinds of energy and qualities involved. All shared the need to be able to hold the space alone, have good timing, physicality and control. Energetically, however, they varied between the high-octane fuelled energy of Charnock to the lower key, controlled rhythm of Houstoun. Etchells comes in low to the ground, casual and subtly menacing, Kimmings is friendly, funny, sharp and direct. Pearson is helpful, a guide, a demonstrator, enabler and family raconteur, Baker uncomfortable, awkward, funny and sharp. One persona works no better than the others – all work within the mix of the rest of the performance. All, however, must ultimately use great skill and control to perform alone, even when the performance signals a chaos. Kimmings and Houstoun spoke of developing their work further through performing it – Kimmings with precise questionnaires, Houstoun with feedback from fellow artists afterwards.

All the practitioners share a commonality as a set of people deeply absorbed in issues of their time, engaging with the world they live in and current problems and possibilities, ranging from issues of women's role in society to sexual disease, mental health, disappearing landscapes, child poverty, duality and existence, and include the subject of performance itself, its limitations and possibilities, They all reveal a clear vision within their work, as well as abilities to collaborate with friends, experts, and their audiences. They are all committed to specific detailed working, enjoying the precision that solo working affords. They all spoke of a deep awareness of their audiences' needs, desires, and live responses and interact with them in numerous ways, from mental to physical interaction.

Some Key Points from the Interviews

My own research into the specifics of the solo-making context was hugely enriched by these interviews, where distinctions, problems, enjoyments and challenges particularly facing solo makers were discussed. The work confirmed my hunch that solo making was not an individual and isolated way to make work but part of a systemic method of performance production, connected to working with others and aesthetic, disciplinary, economic, and political concerns and practices. They revealed some shared challenges around the need to simultaneously be deviser, director and performer, and related questions of distance and closeness to their work, the need to guard against accusations of narcissism or self-indulgence or conversely, the tendency of audiences to always make autobiographical readings of the performance. Issues of finance, time, and space were on-going concerns. Conversely, all enjoyed the solitude, contemplative space, and silence offered by solo working. Self-authorship and self-direction were also valued, as offering the ability to be precise, 'no slippage' in making your own decisions.

What also emerged from this study were numerous examples of particular skills that expert solo performance makers need in order to work effectively. These include the ability to multi-task or orchestrate simultaneous working, be both inside creative working and have a perspective on it, cope with ambiguous situations, avoid closing down questions and curiosity too early in a creative process, have an acute awareness of audience, and enjoy working alone and with others. There are many more.

Choice of Interviewees and the Interview Process

The interviews that follow focus on talking about making, with the practitioners themselves. My choice of interviewees was based on people whose work I enjoyed and also found challenging. As far as one can, in a tiny sample, I took into account geography, gender, ethnicity and diversity of formal working and discipline. I chose to focus on UK-based practitioners as my own practice is based in this context and I also wanted to limit the historical, economic or political differences so as to be better able to focus on artistic questions. I chose practitioners who had a considerable body of solo work already completed, to be able to benefit from their expertise and experience and to also have some basis for comparison. I also wanted to keep the gender balance as even as possible. I am acutely aware that the ethnicity of the interviewees became unfortunately limited to white European. Given that my own performance work and research is specifically about mixed ethnicity and what it can perform, this was frustrating. I approached several BAME practitioners (Anna Deveare Smith, Mojisola Adebayo, Stacey Makishi) but for various reasons it was not possible to include them in this book. However, through the Solo Contemporary Performance Forum I work to increase access, opportunity and the profiles and presence of BAME practitioners, and this work will and does continue.

My invitation in the interviews was towards reflection and this musing involved many moments of pausing, thinking, hesitancy or wondering, often phrased as 'I think', 'perhaps', 'maybe' as well as several moments of new realisation evident in the transcriptions. However because of space limitations, and reading fluency, I have had to edit out many of the pauses or the 'I think' moments, which may lessen the musing-like quality of the spoken interview. It was important to take time. I interviewed each practitioner twice, with at least a space of a month between interviews and each person spoke with me on average for five hours. For this book, I needed to carry out major editing – reducing two interviews into one, reducing the word count and gathering some subject matter into similar areas. I also made slight changes to allow the spoken words to make as much sense when read.

Organisation of the Book

The book comprises seven chapters; an introduction followed by a chapter for each interviewee. Each one is prefaced by an introduction to the practitioner, which aims to provide a brief sketch of what they are particularly known for, some points that came out of their interviews, which I found interesting and a chronology of their solo performance history.

There is no particular logic to the ordering of the series of interviews, apart from a sense I have of putting different perspectives alongside each other. I have included some notes at the end of each section, to identify people the practitioners referred to by first name and what they do, as well as to signal some further readings that may be of interest.

Endnotes

1. Stevens, G. Alexander. 1765. 'The celebrated LECTURE on HEADS', Skinner Row, Dublin: J. Hoey, p. iii.
2. In sixteenth- and seventeenth-century London, England, only two theatre companies were licensed to perform, working in theatres chartered by the King under royal patent: The Theatre Royal (later Drury Lane) and its rival, Lincoln's Inn Fields. Early practitioners like Samuel Foote and Stevens worked around this ban by performing at unusual times, like in the morning, or changing the reason for meeting from performance to social pursuit: 'come and drink a dish of chocolate' (14).
3. John Frohnmayer, fifth Chairman of the National Endowment for the Arts, was responsible for vetoing funding for their work. This decision was later overturned in 1993, after the case was heard by the US Supreme Court and the artists were given the monetary equivalent of the funding. However, this ruling led to Congress advising the NEA to halt its funding of individual artists.
4. Eremitage does also take place in the world; hermits also engage with people and help the poor, so it can be both solitary but also with a social purpose and at times interactive. Solo practice, in this sense, can serve a community of people.

5. Melrose, S. 2007. 'Still Harping On About Expert Practitioner-Centered Modes of Knowledge and Models of Intelligibility'. Keynote presentation at the *AHDS Conference: Digital Representations of Performing Arts*, National e-Science Centre, Edinburgh, July 1–22.

6. Deveare Smith, A. 2005. *Four American Characters*. TED talk. See https://www.ted.com/talks/anna_deavere_smith_s_american_character.

7. A famous exhibition being the 1938 'Exposition international du surrealism at the Galleries Beaux-Arts at 140, Rue du Faubourg Saint-Honoré in Paris, whose exhibitors included Salvador Dali, Marcel du Champ, and Man Ray and which exhibited objects, inventions (Dali's taxi, where visitors were watered, repeatedly) and early installations such as the 'Surrealist Street' (Lehmann, 2008: 66). This is not providing a gloss for 'event art works'.

8. Kaye (1994: 2) locates UK performance art as being more linked to radical theatre practice and feminist work, compared to the focus in the USA on fine arts practices. However, Carlson (2007: 127) writes about the convergence of spoken word, autobiographical, political monologic performance art that existed both in the USA and the UK, from early performance art practices in the 1950s onwards. He suggests these more text-based, political works are often ignored in discourses on performance art that emphasis the abstract visual art qualities (Feral, 1992).

9. Phelan, P. 1993. *Unmarked: The Politics of Performance*. London: Routledge, p. 16.

10. For more detail on the postdramatic, see Lehmann, H.T. 2006. *Postdramatic Theatre*. London: Routledge.

Bryony Kimmings

Bar (2011) ©Christa Holka and Bryony Kimmings

Bryony Kimmings is a self-confessed 'title slag', describing herself alternately as a comedian, 'artist', 'activist', 'playwright' or 'performance artist' – using whatever is needed to get her work known. Like other practitioners in this book, she is a polymath and does not limit herself to working with one particular performance media. Since graduating in Drama in 2003 from Brunel University, she has worked across cabaret, theatre, dance, music and video. She performs both alone and with others in duets, trios and groups.

Kimmings works frequently with highly personal autobiographical material, yet reveals a very light touch in how she deals with this. Her live artwork manages to be both challenging and accessible, and witty and political. She focuses on 'outing' difficult personal and social issues, ignoring the silencing and privatising that often occurs around uncomfortable subject matter such as mental illness, cancer, alcoholism, child poverty, or sexually transmitted diseases. She epitomises the artist who works across the experimental and the popular, allowing for a rich co-existence of both. This is useful for solo performance and Live Art as a genre, preventing it from being pigeon-holed and moving it into a more public, accessible arena.

As such, she has an unashamed eye for promotion and perfectly illustrates a solo artist in control of her public image. This includes the mediated pictures on her website, incorporating airbrushed, luscious images of all her works.[1] The aesthetic achieved is rich, camp, sensual, explicit and bright.

I discussed with Kimmings most of her solo works made to date, and touching upon her early cabaret work. She described this early performance work as including 'meat striptease, B movie poetry, stupid cover songs and naff dances... I would say I was a club kid who made cabaret work in a queer context'. It clearly laid the foundations for what she returns to in her theatre work, namely her use of humour, music, objects, self-ridicule and a camp, at times trashy, aesthetic.[2]

Kimmings was able to talk explicitly and fluently about her making processes in interview and revealed her strong sense of humour and vivid imaginative life. She is not unusual in using her autobiographical history but is not afraid to focus on explicit, shameful personal experiences, laugh at herself and thereby make connections with an audience's own hidden experiences. She described a strong interactive relationship with her live audience, reading them continually in performance (indicative of her stand-up comedy background). She also specifically drew my attention to how important they were to her compositional process, in that she continues to use their written feedback in early showings of all her works, via questionnaires.

Like Baker, Kimmings exemplifies the strong, individual vision of solo devisers who also work as auteurs, writing their own work. She called herself a 'cunt' for not wanting to collaborate more, but then discussed important on-going collaborative relationships which feed into the vision of her work and spoke of these with pleasure and ease. Solo devisers like Kimmings consult others, and then decide themselves. Unashamedly.

She spoke in interview of making processes that demonstrated the experienced practitioner's ability to 'devise' in her head, to conjure up the right source ingredients for a scene (guns and head banging) without necessarily having to try them out.[3] She also gave a useful example of the particular kind of working script that devisers use: 'This next scene is a battle and it looks like all is lost and then it is not.'

Her blog '*I'll Show you Mine*' and the responses to it launched her work as a limited company. She is refreshingly transparent about her economic struggle, and I have included our brief discussion of her finances in order to start to offer transparent examples of charging structures and strategies as deployed by artists.

Performance Chronology

For most of her twenties, Kimmings produced dance and cabaret. From 2009 to 2011 she was employed half time as executive director of Chisenhale Dance Space and half time self-employed. She performed at and ran club nights like *Celebrityville* and *Chisenhale Art Club* at venues such as Chisenhale Dance Centre, Bethnal Green Working Men's Club, Soho Revue Bar and live art and music festivals. In 2010 she made her first theatre piece, the studio-based autobiographical narrative *Sex Idiot*, followed in the same year by *Double Dare*, an interactive, participatory piece performed both alone and with performance artist Jess Latowicki. In 2011, she performed a studio-based, seven-day 'controlled experiment', *7-Day Drunk*; a solo audio walk for audiences, *Mega*; and an installation gallery piece, *The Hall of Gratuitous Praise*. In 2012, she was one of a trio of performers in her ten-minute piece for ten audience members, *Kablooey*; the endurance piece duet, *A Date with the Night*; and a participatory piece for one audience member, *Mummy Time* – sited in a family kitchen above a London nightclub. She was also invited to workshop an idea in Culturgest, an arts festival in Portugal as part of the Scottish live arts organisation Forest Fringe's mini festival. This resulted in *Heartache, Heartbreak*, a theatre piece where she performs 105 solutions offered by strangers as to how to deal with her then failed relationship. 2013 and 2014 saw her creating and performing her perhaps best-known studio work, the duet *Credible Likeable Superstar*, from material devised and performed with her niece Taylor and the follow-on show for young people: *That Catherine Bennett Show*. At the time of interview (2015–2016), Kimmings was performing *Fake It Til You Make It*, a studio work in which she explores the issues of male mental health and depression experienced by her partner, Tim, who also performs (albeit primarily silently) in the work.

Artist website: http://www.bryonykimmings.com/

The Interview

MD: Your first piece, *Sex Idiot*, which you made with Escalator,[4] was autobiographical work. Why?

BK: I wouldn't have thought of anything else. All the artists I liked were from that background. Stacey Makishi[5] had agreed to be my mentor. It was the one thing I knew about. I had no idea about writing character. I wouldn't have known how to make a dance piece because I wasn't a choreographer. I wouldn't have thought of anything else. I came from that background. All the artists I liked were, so I would have made something that just copied everyone else. All I felt like I had the confidence to talk about was my own life. That is the work I enjoy – people talking about their lives. I guess that comes from my background in stand-up.

MD: Can you remember how you got your idea?

BK: I was going out with a guy who was a visual artist and he had a studio. I was quite excited by that. I hadn't come from a visual art background. There was a confidence in that approach, to making work that was alien to me. This idea that you are the artist, and you have a practice. There was something seductive in that that I hadn't seen in more 'theatery' people, writing fictional dialogue. I think I had this weird aspiration to be someone that had a craft and a voice that was original. I remember someone at the Junction asking me 'What do you want to make a show about?' and me saying 'I want it to be somewhere between stand-up, cabaret and performance art. I want to be talking as myself. I have got this story that I think could be provocative but also exciting. I had got chlamydia and I wanted to find out who had given it to me. Everyone I spoke to said 'You can't talk about that', and I thought 'well I don't mind talking about that at all. Why is it so strange that I would sit in the pub and ask all my bird mates if they had had chlamydia?' I was really shocked at how different my perspective at sharing that information was to everybody else's. I just said to the Junction, 'If I am going to make anything at the moment, the only thing I can think about is this. So I will go into my studio and if I have told you I am going to make a show about bananas, I won't be thinking about bananas. I will be thinking about which f****** wanker gave me this thing. So I just thought, if my life is consumed *with* that thing, and everything I am thinking about that is creative is coming *from* that thing, then naturally my practice should be *about* that thing.

So I went into the studio with props and emails from people and everything just felt really right. Dedicating a small piece of performance to anybody that helped me on the real-life journey of finding out about who had given me chlamydia. It felt really rich. That was the first time I went into the studio and felt like 'I have a practice, I have a method'. The method was so rudimentary but it forms the beginning of everything I make and how I make it now.

MD: A method which someone might call research, or exploration or curiosity? You said you go into the studio with some emails, so you had obviously been collecting them before that?

BK: Collecting. Mining. Yeah, research. But it was interactive because they were pieces of performance dedicated to people. So there was an element of storytelling that would naturally be before the act: I will tell the story of Steve and then I'll do the thing I made for Steve and then I'll move on. It was like cabaret, because that is what I knew. There are seventeen stories and with each story we learn something and in each story the character changes. It grows, becomes more self-aware, becomes more ashamed, whatever these stories do to me as a 'character', then it is like a cabaret but it is one person's story. It seemed interesting and like the right thing to do for that show. It was chatty. With the first few showings (which weren't necessarily amazing quality, they were so shit and so DIY and crap) but I discovered it was funny and it was raw and real. I started to perform it a lot, as Stacey and I decided that since I had such low confidence in terms of audience, we should always do a sharing after every performance. Also if I had spent a week in a studio, we would do a sharing. People just liked my personality and language. Everything came from chance. It wasn't premeditated, like I am going to be hilarious, I am going to be feminist, I am going to be feisty, people are going to really appreciate that I am being honest. It was just being myself and I think it was really valuable, because it has not gone away. Like I am now struggling to find how I write, without being in shows. One of the arms of what I am doing now is to write for other people and [when] the strength is the personality of the person performing, how do you populate the stage with 100 Bryonys and keep what everyone loves about my work there? It's weird.

MD: Can I just go back to some basics? So you had some objects and some emails and then you go into the studio, as you said, with what feels like a practice already. You had been doing this activity. Then what did you do?

BK: The objects were selected for their aesthetic beauty and I knew that a lot about the work would be about its visual identity. There were a lot of shamanistic feathers and weird ritualistic objects. They were quite curated, but for no other reason than it felt right to have them. It felt like a purging, this whole exercise. Then I would take the information that I had been given by a person – let's say Steve. He had contacted me and invited me to his house. He had been an agoraphobic when I was going out with him. His house was really far away from mine and I had been a bit pissed off about having to go all this way, and then realised that ten years later, he was still in the same cycle of behaviour that he had been in for a long time. We sat and chatted about how we had broken up and how rough it had been, how I had cheated on him and how hurt he had been. We had a long recorded conversation, putting quite a lot of demons to bed. I said to him, 'let me make you a piece of art' and he said to me: 'I'd like you to try and encapsulate how horrible and beautiful it could be, when we were together'. So I just picked up a bunch of flowers, on the way into the studio. The act was really simple. I had this recording and I listened to it and cried and thought about him and what had happened. I just wanted to make a really short piece, with a long introduction and

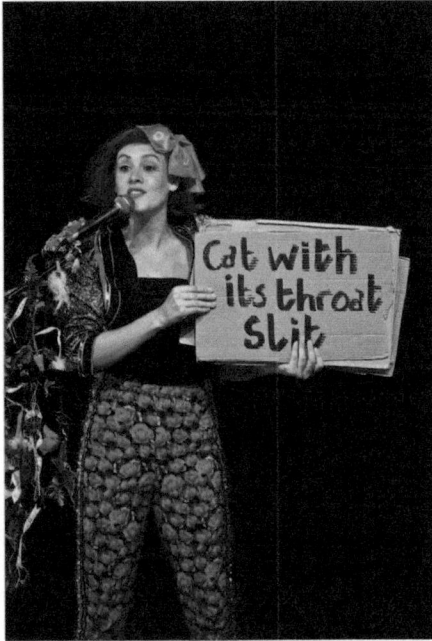

Fanny Song in Sex Idiot (2010) ©Liquid Photo and Bryony Kimmings

story, and then a piece that lasted maybe six seconds. It felt right to do something really short after such a long, protracted story. So I just smashed the flowers over my head, really violently and the piece was called 'The Headfuck of going out with Steve Morris'. It is still the best part of that show. It is so unexpected for it to be that short, unexpected for something so beautiful to become so violent and destructive. So I guess it was like 'How do I encapsulate how I felt about that person or the result of the dirty things that we did to each other? With these objects, what is the best object for that person? Why that act with that object?' So they just came to life on their own a bit. Then the other one everyone always talks about in that show is the pube moustache, where everyone in the audience gives their pubes and I wear them as a moustache – I become somebody with a moustache, the person that I ended up finding out gave me chlamydia. He thought it was so gross that I had slept with so many people. It was like an act of defiance, really. To say, actually, all of these people in this room have also slept with loads of people or done terrible things to one another in secret times. So let's all get our pubes out and let's all f****** recognise for one moment that we are all animals. I will wear them on my face and say that I have no regrets. So it was like, what act encapsulates that story point or at least the feeling or the decision that came from having considered that moment in your life?

MD: You have the stories and the actions and then there is putting them together – composition. What did you do next?

BK: I started to just string them together haphazardly as they were made, first of all, and do these sharings, which I still do now. Because I sit in the studio and imagine lots of things. Then I have to figure out if they technically work. I feel like without showing them, you don't really know if they are actually any good. So I started to just string them all together. But they seemed to work best chronologically, starting from the beginning and coming up to the present day. Because I found it was the man that I was in love with in the present that had given it to me. He had lied. So it felt like that had to be the ending. That it would be the last place you would ever look. It just became more and more nuanced. Like that is better after that one. There has always got to be a sad bit, and straight afterwards I really like to snap to something totally different. I like to stuff things together and see how they fit in front of a live audience. I didn't feel confident and I knew I had Edinburgh coming up, so I did about ten festivals: half an hours, or an hour or two-hour pieces. Each time, a bit like a musician, I just changed the set list a bit. I felt my way through it. Then I did Edinburgh. Because you do twenty-five [performances], the work became nuanced. Beginning to layer stuff. There are lots of layers in my work. They often come quite late. Then I met Nina Steiger, who is the associate director of Soho [Theatre]. When I got back from Edinburgh, they said they wanted to programme it. But she said she wanted a dramaturgical meeting with me, which I had never done before.

MD: Can I just interrupt you? When you say you started 'to layer', what does that mean in terms of what you actually did?

BK: There are two things going on. You say something one night 'off the cuff'. It becomes something that you want to say each time and then you realise that if you don't come back to that two or three times during the show, you are missing a trick in terms of theme or another layer of meaning that you perhaps didn't think of. So let's say, with *Sex Idiot*. In the last two years it has become more of a popular term to say 'slutshaming'. It became a shorthand for something that I didn't have the language for, during the first few runs. I said 'slutshaming' early on in the show and I did a movement with it. That movement comes back two or three times, at the end of something where you may have forgotten or be judging me as that kind of slut. But you may have forgotten that we had already told you that this is about the disgustingness of slutshaming. Often it is movement that becomes the last layer. I have realised in the show I am doing at the moment that I have begun to use this quite stern 'finger point' a lot. It keeps coming back. I put it in something else last night: people pointing fingers at people all the time. It just becomes an extra layer of meaning. So, one is things that naturally come 'off the cuff'. Then other things are 'this show is too funny' or 'this show is too X'. 'There is no counterpoint to this scene'. 'You have been playing it so many times'. 'It's kinda cool but it is really hard to get them back to being serious at this point in the show'. I struggle with that every night. What layer do you add which keeps on bringing us back to the serious? You have played it so many times you need to add in this extra thing. I guess that is what I mean by layers. Also for me, a lot of what I do is looking in to the eyes of human beings who are staring at me. I can see in their faces if it is not the right moment to say something, or if they need something. I can tell from how they are laughing or how they are moving as a group in a darkened room, what they need. It is a bit like stand-up, my practice. The crowd are the most important thing. You can feel how they drop off, or they are struggling. 'I kind of know what she means but I am kind of laughing half because I also don't.'

MD: Yes. In solo, the audience are the only other people in the room, as opposed to speaking to other characters or performers. So that was your first piece. Can we move onto discussing your other work?

BK: *7-Day Drunk* was a solo.[6] I don't particularly like that show. But it was the next big thing that I made. It was about my relationship, and the relationship of my then housemate, to alcohol. Mine was of the pseudo-arty liberal kind, that part of the world is to be this bourgeois drink- and drugs-addled human, a kind of Bokowskiesque fantasy that all artists in their twenties probably buy into. Amy's was much more a really terrible, paralysing alcoholism.

MD: Amy was your flatmate.

BK: Yes. I guess it was about two young women who have both bought into this masculine ideal of what it meant to be an artist. She was a writer, had alcoholism in her family and was a bad alcoholic. It was about why people drink, why we don't ask questions of that, but mostly it was about 'how do I save her? She needs saving, she is turning to me.' There was another performer in that show. Amy was in it only via video because she was in rehab at the time I was making it. But the other performer is an audience member, who plays Amy and gets increasingly more and more hammered, because we give her eleven shots of vodka at the beginning of the show. She becomes an object of ridicule, but in the end, also the perfect example of the problem. It was a weird time because I was trying to make it exactly how I had made *Sex Idiot*, which is a mistake all artists make. So I knew I had seven days to make the show because I had given myself a very strict, experiment-based time limit: seven days to get increasingly more and more drunk in a scientifically controlled environment, in collaboration with scientists. I was only ever allowed to use the material that was generated on days one to seven to create the show that would then be peppered through with the story of Amy and I. Then another layer would be this girl that would get more and more drunk throughout the show. But [I used] object work, making stuff in response to research. I sat in a studio each day from ten to six with an audience each evening and tried to generate material, but didn't have what I had for *Sex Idiot*, which was story. I had actual research – boring and dry. That was a shame. Some people say it was the best show I have made but I felt like I had made the mistake of thinking that that is how you make art… So that was a solo…

…*Mega*[7] was just an exploration. I loved writing stories and I wanted to tell a story of my youth that I really liked, which was about this restaurant that came to my town that was shaped like a spaceship. This weird restaurant in my tiny little fen town that I grew up in, in St Ives,

Seven Day Drunk (2011) ©Liquid Photo and Bryony Kimmings

in Cambridgeshire, near Peterborough. This extraordinary thing had happened. This American air base had descended on a town nearby and someone thought it was a good idea to build a spaceship-shaped restaurant on the side of the road. Everybody in my school got to go. But being from a poor, single-parent family, we never went. We were not allowed. It was £8 for a meal, which was a lot of money at the time. I was just getting really upset about child poverty. It was the beginning of reading stuff in the papers and feeling so angry. Then making things in response to the way I felt about something which is much, much more my practice now. Less biography and much more social injustice and activism, I suppose. It was just a really simple story. It took me about twenty minutes to write it. I didn't know what I was going to do with it. It was just about the day we got to go.

MD: When you say you wrote it, did you sit with a pad and paper or did you use a computer?

BK: Yes, I wrote it with a computer. Just a stream of consciousness but I knew that I wanted to write it as if … I wanted to transport the person. I thought it would be read, maybe that it would be audio recorded, but I wanted the person that was listening to it to be me, to try to remember what it was like to be nine, but also to be me at nine. How can you persuade or convince a reader or a listener that actually, in the click of a finger, you are going to be nine again? You are going to be a girl and you are going to be poor and you are going to have a shit life. You are going to remember that moment. You are going to listen to the moment where a young girl realises she is growing up and that life is shit and it's always going to be shit unless you do something about it. That moment where the shine comes off your youth, which of course is never encapsulated in one moment.

MD: And your question was how can you make the listener experience that, through a re-performing of what?

BK: Two things. (1) That they can imagine themselves in that scenario. (2) That they can also remember being that age and what it was like for them. So it was important that there was a kind of duality to the experience. You are now nine and you are Bryony Kimmings and its 1990 and you are going to experience what she had to experience at that moment. You are going to try your best to understand how awful that might have been. But at the same time you are also going to be your 9-year-old self too, because you will be thinking about yourself at nine and what that was like. It was the conflict between those two things that became really fascinating. It was never the intention that people would come back from that experience and say 'Oh poor Bryony' but rather weep for their own lost childhood. Weep for their own moment when they remember the shine coming off.

MD: That aim makes for the best autobiographical work, I think. Work that is finely detailed about a moment in time, with the point being to trigger in an audience a remembering of their own moments.

BK: That is all our job is really – to use our stories to make people think of theirs. None of the stories in *Sex Idiot* are so profound that they would ever change your life but they will make you think about all the shit things you have done and all the things you want to say sorry for. So *Mega* was a really lovely way to start to realise you could get tactical with that and really raw. It was simple. Then the idea became – 'ok, well this would be cool to listen to through a Walkman because I remember having a Walkman at the time and I mention a Walkman in the show. Wouldn't it be cool to listen to it on tape because tape sounds so reminiscent of that time? Wouldn't it be cool to intersperse that Italia 90 song or "rhythm is a dancer"'? Moments where you don't want text for a while. Pauses. There are a lot of pauses in the script, that say 'pause 15 seconds'. So we filled them with either space just to think or space for music and then it was like 'you don't wanna be seated in a room with other people looking at you. You wanna be walking around a council estate'. The layers started to come. 'You want to be walking around a council estate. You want to be dressed in a shell suit and listening to your Walkman'. In every possible physical way, try to make that person nine again.

MD: When you say you want to be doing this, can you remember if that was a visual image in your head?

BK: Well, it was a commission. It was gonna happen and it was like – do I want people to read this on a piece of paper, do I want people to listen to this in the room? No, I want people to be dressed in a shell suit, walking around a council estate listening to this, to try and transport them somehow back into 1990, to help them get to that state.

MD: I am interested to push that a bit, as to whether that is an idea or a visual image? For me, it would have been a visual image, imagining a person walking around.

BK: It wouldn't have been that for me. It would have been an imagining of being a person listening to it. I would listen to it and think, that is not enough. What if that person was sitting in a café? No, that is not right. What if that person was somehow in a spaceship? No that would be shit because it would be trivial. What of that person was dressed as a girl? Yeah – that is the right option. Thinking about what they would feel like, listening to the piece of work. I think it is more that than visualising it for me. That is a hard question.

MD: Yes, and I am interested in that detail.

BK: You don't think about it yourself, in terms of your own practice. It is interesting to be asked this question. Its instinct. I think that most of my decisions are made putting myself in the position of the audience, I guess…

So the next solo that I made after that was *Mummy Time*.[8] That is the only one-to-one I think I have ever made. After *7 Day Drunk* I was like – 'I am not making that mistake again, of trying to make that same show. So I am going to make lots of different things that seem to match the subject matter. Instead of egotistically driving it forward to make another show, I'll make a lot of stuff where the form will be dictated by the subject matter.' It was a really lovely time because it was very freeing and that's where [I decided] I'm not going to make things because the Arts Council want to see the next application for the next Bryony Kimmings show. I'm going to make things only about the things I want to talk about and then I'm going to choose the form because of the subject matter, not because of my ego. It was a really shit time. I made no money, because I made the one-to-one and an audio piece. I had moved home with my mum, and left Chisenhale. It was a classic M.A. but a self-inflicted one. I had gone 'oh do you remember the boyfriend that was a visual artist and he had his room and he knew so much about what each thing should be, because he had considered it so finitely'. I was like 'I want that, I want that practice'. So *Mummy Time* – I was in it sometimes and sometimes I wasn't in it but I would say it was a solo because it was about my life.

MD: How did that piece start?

BK: It was a time when I was being much closer to my family. This is where *'Credible'* [my later show and] – probably the most successful piece that I made – came from. It was a lot about considering family and thinking about autobiography in that way. It was a really small one-to-one piece where you come into a room that is set up like a council flat, and you are thrust into a scenario where a mother is busy drug dealing but also ironing. She had an ironing business and a heroin racket going on with the rest of the family. Again, you become a child. I think the idea was you were around five or six. You have been picked up by your sister from school. That is how you are met, by your older sister, brought home and given a shit tea of Wotsits and ham sandwiches. Then a rush phone call came in for a big order and so instead of doing your homework, you would have to wrap up all of the heroin with your sister, sitting there with your little hands and doing it. Then right before getting the order ready and the mum barking all the different instructions to you, a social worker would come and rip you out of the scenario. So you were flung into this awful place and then ripped out of it again. It was very quick, about five minutes long. It's not my autobiography; it's the auto-biography of someone on my estate who I had rekindled a friendship with.[9] I remember going round their house, remembering that mother and remembering that scenario for that child. They did get taken into care. I was thinking about how that must have felt for that kid. People don't think that that happens, but it happens a lot. So I just wanted to honour that person's story by making something fierce and beautiful but also really tragic. So you are the protagonist in the story, even though you are five. I think one-to-ones always pissed me off because they are always a bit like 'oooh hold my hand in the dark'. F*** off, why can't one-to-ones be like 'did you know that people's parents use to deal heroin while they were eating their Rice Krispies and they had to wrap heroin before they came to school?' There will probably be kids in your school that had to do that. Why do one-to-ones always have to be twee experiences? No – you come out the other side of that one-to-one and you can't breathe.

MD: Did you have the same creative process in making that as the other pieces? You had said 'No, I am going to let the form come from the content'.

BK: I had an idea to immerse someone in a very chaotic life for five minutes and then chuck them out the other side. Brian Lobel curated it as part of a night that he used to do called 'Cruising for Art'. He ran them all over the place. He did one at Vogue Fabrics in Dalston, and Lyle's flat was above the club there and he said, 'I have got this flat and you can smoke in it and you can do what you want in it.' It was really important to me that that whole room was filled with fag smoke. Brian said, 'why not just try it?' I loved it. It was the first time I had ever gone, 'Ok (there was another performer in it with me – a younger sister, a 16-year-old performer) what we're going to do is – we have got this clock on this wall and we have got five minutes and this is the story. The friend is going to ring and I'm going to be ironing, it's not going to be scripted.

You're going to bring the kid in, see if they've got homework, the kid gets to improvise (the kid being the audience member obviously). You chat a bit, the phone rings and everything changes. They have to try and make these wraps with you and you have to show them how to do it. They have to measure out the heroin and they have to weight it. Then there is a knock on the door and the other performer (the social worker) is going to come in and they are going to improvise the scene. Then the young person is going to get chucked out the other door.' Because it was a club night it was fine. We did about twenty-five of them. By the end it was like 'ah that's what's good about them'. We just changed it each time. I would say, 'ok don't say that, it doesn't sound genuine when you say heroin, we don't call it heroin, we call it horse' or whatever. The information for that came from long in-depth conversations with my friend. So I knew the language, the scenario: the mother, the daughter, I knew them all. So it was kind of about trying to imagine that scenario and then once that was done I could hand that over as a script. I typed it and then I could rehearse it and people did it where I wasn't the mum. In fact we did it once where the girl whose life it was was the mum, which was really nice.

MD: That reminds me of certain classic kinds of drama therapy techniques. Not that your intention is therapeutic but in work that I've done before where a real-life scenario is re-enacted.

BK: The feedback from that show was really interesting. I didn't think it was that good, that show, but people loved it and it was really strange. I think it was to do with either 'poverty porn' – feeling cool because you've done something cool – or a curator that really loved that show said 'people never really thought about that before' and then he couldn't not think about it ever again. He couldn't look at kids that looked a bit dirty on the street and not think 'I wonder what the f*** is going on behind that door'. I thought that was much better than the poverty porn element to it.

MD: And you made seven pieces in one year?

BK: Yeah. I just put my head down. I was lucky that I was an associate artist at The Junction, so there were often festivals and there was loads of escalator stuff going on. I was quite popular at the time – people thought 'Ooh, whose this new bird?' I think there are less opportunities now but there was loads of stuff you could always do. So I was making one-offs, a bit like my friend Richard Dedominici (he was the only other artist that I really knew). Obviously after that year I thought 'well that is not a sustainable practice in any way, shape or form' but it was delightful. That is why I think of it as my M.A. I learnt a lot. I learnt that the most important thing was to make something that you give a s*** about. Then I made *Credible*.

MD: Not '*Heartache Heartbreak*?[10]

BK: Oh yes – I made that. That was back to the object work actually. I had got to a festival in Portugal, with Forest Fringe. There were three of us as artists that were there to workshop ideas and about seven other people who were doing shows. So we had a week to come up with something. I had never done that before. I was terrified. You have a week and then you have to show something, which of course I had done in my own practice but not with such a furious deadline. I had got dumped, so all I wanted to do was sit in a hotel and cry. I didn't want to make stupid art. I was heartbroken. I spent four days crying, walking around the city. I was slightly surprised at how many people come to your aid in a foreign country, when you sit on a bench and cry. It was quite an old area, full of old people. So they would say 'what is the matter with you?' I would say 'I have had my heart broken' and they would say these phrases or pieces of advice, really well trodden like, 'Oh you know, you'll get over it' or 'I had my heart broken forty years ago and I never got over it'. Then I started to provoke those scenarios, so I'd go into shops and cry and then ask the person behind the counter, 'Give me some advice, I am dying of heartache'. It became a kind of game. I started to enjoy the conversations and I thought 'this is the only thing that is coming out of this research that seems to be interesting: the unification of two human beings over the act of being heartbroken and the way it softens communication between people'.

So I went back to my roots of *Sex Idiot* and I recorded them and took them back to the studio that I was working in and made a piece for every single person that had given me advice. Antonio in the pipe shop had said 'just get over it, stop crying, stop being such a pussy' so I made a piece of work for him. They were all word plays, because there was a lot of miscommunication from English to Portuguese. There was something really interesting going on with language and sayings. So 'just get over it' was pulling someone out of the audience, putting a sticker on him, saying his name was 'it' and then trying to climb physically over him. Ways of messing with language and laughing at love and heartbreak and reclaiming oneself. 'It takes time' – so then we would have to get that guy who was 'it' again to steal the clock from the room. I then invited all of those people that had helped me to come and watch the show. So it was like the Portuguese Barbican basically, with all these really posh people, and then in my room there were all these shopkeepers and flower store sellers. It was wicked. So they had got this little tiny piece and I think there was about 105 pieces in the show and it was just played out – 105 sure-fire ways to get rid of heartache. Then I did it again and again and I really liked the process of it.

MD: In terms of composition, 105 moments must have been endless – rolling out bang bang bang bang bang. Was that the point?

BK: That was what it was. It was the multiplicity of it all that made it so ridiculous and made the heartache so pointless by the end. There was the story of having my heart broken and the first few play out and are really important and then it starts to be like, oh s***, we have got sixty-five left and its already half an hour in and how are we going to cram them in? It started to become manic, ridiculous, people started to have to do them for you. So you got this tick list and then by the act of belittling it, it made it a funny comment about love. It was stupid to moan, stupid to talk about it, 'shut up'. By the end of it, it was like, 'I'm fine, I'm actually going to be fine. I've got this out of my system in a really beautiful shared community way'. I did a version of it at The Bush[11] and everyone really liked it, but I never thought of it as a theatre show. But people reviewed it like it was a theatre show. But I thought it as an hour of stand-up really. I did it down the Shepherd's Bush High Road or Uxbridge Rd. I did the same thing – 'I have had my heart broken, what do I do?' I made new pieces of work for all those people as well. It was quite a nice format. It works as a ten-minute piece or a half-an-hour piece.

MD: Where was the first place you performed that?

BK: Culture Jest in Lisbon. I did it in Manchester at the Contact as well and I think I did it in Ipswich.

MD: So then you went onto *Credible, Likeable* with your niece Taylor.

BK: Yeah. That was a massive project and I guess it was a solo? I mean it was a collaboration between me and a 9-year-old kid. I wrote the work but she was in the show.

MD: I would put it into a category that it is solo devised, in collaboration with Taylor, but then performed as a duet…[12]

BK: Ok, so after that, I made *Fake It* – the thing that I am doing now.[13]

MD: So we are up to the present day. *Fake It* is again performed as a duet but devised by you?

BK: It is a 'duet' but primarily written and performed by me because Tim[14] spends most of the show with his face covered. He is anonymous.

Fake It Til You Make It (2015) ©Richard Davenport and Bryony Kimmings

In the last twelve minutes, he becomes Bryony Kimmings in a way and I leave the stage. He takes over the story because he becomes brave enough to take off his mask and to talk. There was something really nice and liberating about that, that he becomes the solo performer in the end.

It is actually Tim's story. Well it's not because it's actually the story of a woman experiencing Tim's story through being his girlfriend but his story is the backbone; the narrative is his eight years of struggle with mental health secretly, and his coming out and then being able to do something positive with that instead of it being so shameful for him. But it was just very obvious when I began working with him that he would never be able to tell his own story. It was too close to everything happening. I was the one who was the writer; I was the one who was the performer. The fact that it was being told by me undermines him to the point where if I carried on talking and he never reveals himself in the show, he would be doing the same thing that he had been doing for eight years. So the device of me running out of words and him finding words was really important. It kind of plays with the form of the solo really nicely, as a concept. I would say on the grounds that you were talking about what solo work is, it is a solo. It's my narrative. I am narrating it. I am telling his story for him until he takes the mantle, it becomes his solo and I go off stage. So it's never really a two hander that solo, because for the whole time until five minutes from the end, he can't tell the story. I do really like it. It's much more complex in terms of real human beings, their emotions, their relationships, their impending birth. It's very real. It's very much like being in a room with two people who are having a relationship and trying to figure out how to have that relationship extremely publicly.

MD: Tell me a bit more about your making process in *Fake It*.

BK: I asked Tim 'give me the rules in which you are happy to do this'. One was 'I am happy to do it, but I can't look anyone in the eye and I don't want to speak'. I didn't have any ideas as I rarely do anyway about what it would end up like. I just go into the studio and start making. We had recorded the entire story of his mental health struggles for eight years, over an hour sitting in our lounge, drinking a bottle of wine. I had sent it to Tom Parkinson, my dramaturg and composer that I work with and it was so raw and obviously very difficult for him, with us two crying a lot. He said, 'That's the story, that's it'. So very early on, I knew the narrative was this snipped up audio track that would replace his voice, which he did not feel like he could use live every night. Then I felt like it would be cool to have his version and then my version of events from the most recent of his breakdowns. Then it was always the same old – 'this will be a song, this will be a dance, this will be a moment, this will be a recording' – it's still the same approach. That's how it was made, in bits, as usual, but I did sit down and write this one. Instead of going to the studio and seeing if this thing would work, I can now know that it does or doesn't.

MD: What would you say is the role of your 'self' in your solo work?

BK: I guess I am soothsayer, confessor, clown – loudest bravest, stupidest biggest, person in the room. I am the fool in my work, the one who knows the least.

MD: Is that something that you have learnt to adopt as a persona, a strategy? Obviously that really relates to comedy doesn't it? Nobody likes a smart-arse comedian.

BK: Yes, and that probably comes from my cabaret background. They have all got to slightly fall in love with you. They can't f****** hate you. You are romancing them, convincing them that slowly but surely, your opinion is valid. That is why there is always a top bit: 'Hi I'm Bryony and these are some things that you probably don't know about me but you should. I am shit at this and I am a liar and I probably buy too much food and chuck it in the bin. I'm awful. I'm not a very good functioning human being' – that kind of thing. So everyone thinks, 'Fine, nor am I, great' as opposed to 'Hi I'm the queen, respect me'. It's definitely a comedy thing, clowning isn't it? You have to have something that makes everybody else feel ok about their something. Everyone's got something that they hate about themselves and it's true especially for women in performance. Maybe with Russell Brand – we feel 'ok he's just this God'. He never self-deprecates, we're meant to see him as a Messiah. But a woman could never pull that off, really annoyingly. I can't think of a single woman or female performer that doesn't come on stage and somehow apologize for trying to get her f****** opinion heard. You kind of have to go with that and understand that that is just human nature.

You can then f*** with that and you can be the person that is the Messiah and they're hanging off your every word, but you have to apologize and win them over first. Which is fine. It's what you have to do when you meet someone in a room. You don't just suddenly go 'Hi I'm Bryony and you are pretty much going to want to be my best friend. I might as well just skip this chat because you're going to wanna hang out with me for the rest of the evening'. You can't! You've got to earn it, haven't you?

MD: You sure do. So with *Fake It*, you were also talking about it as a demonstration of a 'real' relationship performed to the audience.

BK: Yeah, it is 'we are going to talk about our relationship so you can talk about your relationships. We're going to pour our hearts out to you, but it's not so you go "Oh poor Bryony and Tim". It's so you leave and think, "oh I need to do something about x or y, I need to phone so and so"'. When I'm making a piece of work, the audience intention is written on the wall of the studio in blood. In *Credible* it was 'they have to f****** cry their eyes out, mourn for their lost childhood and leave wanting to do something about the world instead of sitting watching f****** Netflix'. With every decision that's made, I ask 'Is this doing this? Is this happening? Are we allowing people to see themselves in it? Is it too navel gazing?' For the Tim show it was for men to leave not feeling ashamed of their mental illness. How do you use our story and filter in key points where the audience are going to realise and change something? You are manipulating them f****** hard. Especially with this show, everybody is crying by the end. I am f****** crying by the end. There is something to be said around misery porn which is gross and you don't want to do. All I am doing is picking the right part of the story, which makes people open their eyes about something, I suppose? Which is really rude and a bit presumptuous, but that is why I pick subjects which we don't really talk about, because the question is 'why aren't we talking about this?'

MD: In *Fake It*, who are you in it? What about the power relationships?

BK: It is so layered. That show is extremely complicated. I am myself. I am also my performance self. I am trying to be myself and as honest as possible. But I am also my performance self because I am on the stage, so there is always going to be two different people: the heightened, less boring version. Then there is 'lover', because there are three time zones in that show: the past, the present and the imagined future: the baby in my stomach. I am playing past self; lover and naïve girlfriend. I am playing my current self, who is an artist looking in on my own life and trying to tell that story as an artist. I am also playing myself in all the scenes that are in the past but also currently happening on the stage. And there are often moments in the middle of a scene where I will step out and say, 'Can you imagine this happened?' So I am in and out of different time zones and contexts. Then, I am also responsible for Tim, so I am director and girlfriend and carer. I am also the provocateur of his misery because I am the manipulator of his story for entertainment value. So there are so many roles I am playing in that work and your opinion of me changes so much during that show. 'What a f****** bitch, what an absolute hero, what a total academic with total disregard for his emotions'. You go through so many phases. Because, also, I am playing opposite a blank person. It is like a duet with somebody who isn't really there. But what has been a really lovely realisation is to write the scene from the perspective of the manipulator; to admit that. There is a part in this show where we are backwards and forwards between two mics saying all the things that have happened, like we got a doctor, we got all the books, we got really prepared, we hibernated. And then one of them was 'I secretly had the idea to make this show'. Suddenly you are not in the story anymore, you are the artist. We knew that there were all these different versions of Bryony in the show and not all of them are good people. Some of them are manipulative and some of them are fantasy-imagined versions of what you are like. The only person that is real is Tim when he takes off his mask, because he's not a performer and he's not being anyone apart from a man who has written a speech about his own mental health. But then you've got the problem of one hundred shows in, he also becomes a performer...

MD: Let's talk about collaboration. Who do you collaborate with to make your solo works?

BK: I have always had a team of the same people. David Curtis-Ring[15] does the visuals: costumes, props and sets and it is always a collaboration. I come to him and say, 'the show is totally neon or this show is all flesh coloured' and then we begin and we work brilliantly together. He has worked on every show. The photographs for the show and the airbrushing are Christa and Alex[16] and they are very important because for me the image for the show is just as important as the whole rest of it. The image is always immaculate. To make the actual work, I write on my own for a while because I get very easily swayed. So I make a lot of decisions before I bring anybody in. I wouldn't sit and canvass opinion on the question that I am investigating, for example. I would get that right first. I might have a few conversations with people but I wouldn't let anybody have ownership over the idea. It's normally an idea because it's a pursuit of some kind, so I get that right in my head. Then I will chat to Tom Parkinson, who is weirdly my music collaborator but also my dramaturg. I will chat to him a lot about the subject matter around the show, so he'll know that I'm making something about sexually transmitted infections. He's very intelligent, much more intelligent than me and he's very interesting to talk to and very feminist. Then I will write stuff and it will be Nina Steiger[17] who reads and dramaturgs the writing. Once there [are] two or three drafts in, Tom is allowed to read it. Nina knows what I mean even if I'm not saying it, and I can write into a script 'Scene 3: I don't know what it is yet but it definitely has got to do something that pokes everybody in the eye'. It's got to be a shift moment when you thought you knew what was going on, but you don't. I don't know what that is yet'. Nina will be able to say 'ok, I get that and I can carry on reading and we'll come up with suggestions' whereas Tom would say 'I don't really understand what you mean by that' and so I would find that hard. I don't want to have to explain to him that I don't yet know what that is but somewhere in the back of my mind I do. So he gets it when everything almost hangs together as a narrative and he can say, 'There is a hole here because you have started something there and you haven't finished it'. So it gets more technical. Then I will go into the studio and Tom will go with me. Nina will come to the sharing and so will a few key people who I would probably always invite – other artists. Like I would probably have Brian Lobel there if I could because he is really good at feedback and David [Curtis-Ring], because he would say 'oh you need to have this little peacock'.

MD: So Tom will go into the studio with you in his role as a musician and dramaturg. What does he do?

BK: The last two projects have had non-performers in them so that makes it a bit of a different scenario. He is another expert in the room, helping me look at that person as an object and figure out what is good and bad about them. He has a script, so he knows that by the time we [are] going into the studio for the first time, there is definitely music at the beginning; foreboding, twinkling broken carousel, or whatever. I will bring with me all the ideas of what that scene might look like, because I have imagined it in my head, and no one else knows yet. David might drop in some early costume, or props or objects, and then Tom will come with his stuff. So he will be ready. It's more likely he would go away and make stuff and come back in, and I'd go away and think about it and come back in and we would just jam it together. Often the conversation is as basic as, 'That looks f****** cool' or 'Don't say it like that because you sound up yourself. Why don't you make that line like this? Do you mean this? You are just waffling'. It's like jamming. It's sort of like putting a play on because you get the script and you go through it but often the scripts are like: 'This next scene is a battle and it looks like all is lost and then it is not' and you are like 'oh my God what does that mean?'[18]

So on this particular day [I might say], 'Let's look at headbanging and guns. 'Why'? 'Just because it just seems right today'. 'Ok'. It's as simple as that really,[19] and I really like that, the freedom to say 'Today the battle is head banging and guns and tomorrow it could have been anything else'. You feel your way through, don't you? We find that so fun. It is so beautiful and we get on well and we know exactly what the other one is going to say. So Nina starts to drop out a bit as she is in charge of narrative and red herrings and language and metaphor and that comes from the writing of the text. She has to be the warden of that. When we have been in the studio for a while, she will come back in and say, 'Why is there now suddenly loads of icebergs in it, when it was always going to be the sea? The frozen sea doesn't make sense in those metaphors, take it out. Or you have to change 'it'.' So she is the warden of the more English-language based stuff and Tom is going, 'Oh my God there needs to be a dragon in this moment' and I say 'Why' and he says 'I don't know but let's just get a dragon'. It doesn't seem very organised but it is when we are doing it. Then we would have a sharing with certain people invited to do notes and feedback. Then back in the studio. It would be Tom that was always there. He doesn't get a co-director because he is a dramaturg. That is what he is doing – he is asking questions.

MD: So he is more a dramaturg than a musician.

BK: He does all the music for the show.

MD: Interesting that he is both those things.

BK: It's weird isn't it? But he didn't make the music for *Fake It* actually, not all of it because he wasn't there.

MD: Why doesn't he get a co-director credit?

BK: We have talked about it before. He doesn't because it's ultimately my decision and he is following the whimsy of some f****** idiot most of the time. He is always following me. He would never come into the studio and say 'Ok, scene two, I have had this idea and we should do it like this', never. I wouldn't allow him to. It wouldn't work. He studied at Dartington but he went and lived in Holland for ten years and he is very Dutch. I love that European dance-theatre eye.

MD: With solo work, crediting is an interesting issue. My definition of solo in this book is that solo is primarily the vision of one person – writing, staging and performing. It's really clear, I think, when people switch into something else.

BK: Yes, like an auteur in film.

MD: Are there any particular generic devising strategies you use, across your pieces of work?

BK: Headlines are mostly that it gets shown and workshopped and I get loads of feedback forms and test everything vigorously. It's really the only thing that I think is different to a lot of artists, that sort of paranoid canvassing of public opinion.

MD: So you use specific feedback forms?

BK: I have a specific form because I find scratch or forum feedback or even Liz Lerman[20] is never the truth and is always ego driven or someone is angry about something, or people are being kind. So I always do a form. It is the same form: 'what did you see?' I like that question because if everyone is thinking 'she's a maniac with an axe to grind' and I was thinking 'Virgin Mary trying to tell her story' then I have got the tone wrong! Also, people see very little of what you have done. Because it goes by in the blink of an eye. 'What did you see?' Well, no one saw the knife I was holding. Why not? Why didn't they see that? It needs making bigger. 'What do you want to see more of?' instead of '[w]hat did you like?' and then the opportunity of '[w]hat did you want to see less of?' so people can be harsh and mean: 'We would like to see less Lily Allen and a bit more originality'. Whatever that might be. Then there [are] normally a few specific questions about material. Anything that I am really paranoid about I will put on there. I have got hundreds of them. I keep them all. They are really helpful, I couldn't make work without them, without that process. I can't guess. I get it wrong. For example, for the cancer musical, all of the cancer patients said that they had to see a death. All of them. 'Where's the death?' and I thought 'what the f*** are they talking about?' They said 'Nobody ever does a death well. You always have the heroes' death at the end of a movie but why not just have a shit death and no one is there because that is what the worst bit of cancer. Not the heroes' 'last hurrah' but more like hospice death, a f****** horrible thing and show it, don't not show it. If you don't show it you're avoiding it and that is what everyone is thinking when they have cancer: death – terrible – show it'. I would never have known that. I would have avoided it, maybe.

MD: Earlier when we were talking off record, you said 'after the blog everything changed'. The blog is 'I'll show you mine'. Did you mean it changed economically?

BK: I did. Everything changed because, even in the process of writing it, I thought 'well this doesn't have to be like this – this is just me making it like this', as well as other people forcing that to be the case. Everything changed politically and economically. The first thing that happened was my dramaturg Nina called me up and said, 'Why are you charging £150 a day? Why aren't you charging £350 a day?' I was like 'What?' She said, 'Why aren't you?' and I said, 'Because that is extortionate'. She said, 'Put your fee up and see what happens'. I put my fee up and nobody said anything. So that was amazing in itself. No one f***** with me again, like venues, because it [the blog] got so big so quickly and because so many people read it and got scared. I thought I would lose work. I got more work, paid well and a lot of artists have said that since then, nobody haggles anymore. They got scared. It was funny. I don't think they realised that they were doing it and the damage that the knock-on effect economically had on solo artists. It was the first time someone had said 'I'm not coping. I'm not making any money and it's not cost effective'. So it was a shift, in a really good way. It made me ask 'ok what are the other things I can do?' At the time, I had applied for a big Arts Council organisational development grant to get staff. I was drowning and not earning enough. They came to me and said, 'You know you can apply for money to establish yourself as a company limited and get yourself some staff'. I was like 'Can I?' I had reached the top of solo in terms of sole tradership and it was either, 'This is going to be hard and I am going to earn £16,000 a year or something has to change'.

So everything changed in my practice. I took on a general manager, and an administrator. I started to fundraise. The turnover tripled in a year. I could be an artist and I didn't have to do all the other things. So I made work rapidly. I got an agent, which I had been scared of before. Lots of people wrote to me and said, 'Why don't you do this and why don't you do this' and I thought 'These are all brilliant ideas I'll do them all'. I did a proper business plan with not just arty people and everything did change. But I guess it was because I said 'Oh I am not coping, could somebody help me?' The good thing about the arts is everybody helps everybody, don't they? It was two years ago.

MD: Is your manager funded throughout the year or do they work on projects?

BK: No, they are funded. We earn enough money to pay them. So Jo, the general manager, works two and a half days a week and so does Amy, the administrator. I also have an education project manager for a very specific project for next year, so I do have project stuff as well. Obviously Tom is paid project by project. Tim and I are paid a full-time salary – there are five payroll staff in Bryony Kimmings Ltd so it's a very different thing. It means I have to turn over £7,000 a month just to pay people's wages, a whole different thing but it feels infinitely less scary than it used to feel because it's very organised. It's [planned] a year ahead. We have already got the money, we don't have worries about cash flow, for example. The first year of trading was really difficult. There were lots of times when we thought we didn't have any money to pay wages this month. Now it's ahead of itself, because we have become a company limited and we can apply for much big bigger grants and projects. (This has changed so much now, I have no staff and am broke! But leave it I guess?)

MD: So does your funding come from mainly grants or touring?

BK: Touring. I would say this year commissioning was around £20,000. Touring was around £80,000. I taught four workshops this year – that was £15,000. Merchandise, £2,000. I got a Gulbenkian grant to deliver an education project that was £20,000. I got commissioned to write the musical that was £20,000. We have been asked to write a book and we are fundraising for the boys' project. It depends, but gigs bring in the most money. Jo is now fundraising for the end of next year.

MD: So if I say the word 'solo' to you, what does it conjure up?

BK: It makes me think of dance firstly. Then I think about monologue, soliloquy and all of that. The type of work that I like that is solo would be autobiographical work. I've watched many solo plays and I f****** hate them mostly. Solo dance – I feel ambivalent about because it's just what people do when they have just graduated and they haven't got the budget for dancers. But if it is autobiographical and it is someone talking directly at me, that is probably why I really like it. For me, in terms of performance, solo doesn't equal cheap. But for everything else, it equals cheap for some reason. It's cheap to do a solo, it's easier and convenient, you can get a small studio space. But if it's something confessional and autobiographical, it's important that it's a solo. That's the beauty of it. It's one person confessing or lying or tricking you. I really like solo work when it's done well. I hate it when it's done really badly. The inauthentic copying of something I have seen done by more established artists – it happens a lot doesn't it? Which is fine because most people make something in the style of something and then their work will slowly become in the style of themselves. That is fine. I don't like people talking about stuff that I care little about, which happens a lot. Oh my dog died. Who gives a f***? Or self-indulgent confessing of how crazy someone is. Or that the artist has clearly not put two and two together and understood why that might be actually interesting for the audience. They have just thought 'oh a solo, an autobiographical work is just the telling of my story' and they haven't considered that actually it is not about them, it is totally about the audience. I also find the stringing together of moments that were good in a workshop studio space, without the consideration of why those things marry together nicely, is a problem. What are we trying to say by combining those things in that particular order? It is important to have a shared language. But the amount of times I have seen glittery leotard, helmet running against a wall as some kind of finale. Roller skates ... We did have this joke, a group of artists, about a list of things that it is no longer acceptable to have in a piece of art. Roller skates is one, live Skype conversations is another, they just get worn out, don't they, the tropes?

MD: So that moves nicely into asking you to describe your favourite moment from a piece of solo work that is not your own?

BK: In this solo called *Family Holds Back*, by Helen Paris, one half of Curious – its 2003, maybe 2004. There is a moment in that show where she has been talking about her family history, 'stiff upper lip' and family holding back at the dinner table and all those rules that get in between you and actual conversation with your family. It's a beautiful piece of work and she is a beautiful performer. There is a moment where she is sitting at a table, with a very starched white tablecloth, folding napkins, talking, unfolding them and them becoming other things to illustrate people. Just really simple. Suddenly, she takes the tablecloth off and underneath (everything is very precise and beautifully lit) there is a very shallow, clear plastic tray of very hot water. She pulls off the tablecloth and this steam comes out of it, up into this gorgeous light that is coming down. I can't even remember why it is so poignant. She gets into it and covers herself over and drowns in her words. But it wasn't anything to do with that, it was just the moment that that comes of and this steam comes out. That is my favourite moment in any solo ever. It's weird. It was unexpected, it was beautiful, it was the perfect thing to happen at the perfect moment. It was about ritual, so you know that she has to be clean, she has to get out of all this tangle of this family. I don't know why? It was such a lovely surprise – a beautiful surprise. The steam was so clinical, perfect. I think it was the classiness of it. Everyone went 'ohhhh'.

MD: It's also very 'simple' as an action, isn't it?

BK: Yes – it's so hard to find simple. Everything is embellished. Everything about her story had gone into this moment. It was like the big reveal. She had had her arms on the table, so she must have constantly been only resting her arms. It was magic. It felt magical as a piece of performance.

MD: It's a live thing as well, isn't it? It would be different if that was on film. You are there.

BK: Yeah. The steam! How come that had not been steaming through that beautiful white tablecloth? Yes, it was very live. There is a bit in a Stacey Makishi show where she gives birth to a bunch of brussels sprouts. That would be my second choice, just because she is funny.

MD: Yes, I have been in contact with her for several years. I had hoped she would be part of this book, but she was too busy.

MD: What do you think is particular about solo work?

BK: It's my story, my voice, my life – me, me. In fact I almost made the cancer musical 'Bryony Kimmings goes and interviews loads of people about cancer and then this is what she realises about mortality'. But I just thought that that was too boring. I don't know what is particular about solo.

MD: Ok, what is particular about *making* solo?

BK: It's a dictatorship. That is it. There is no relinquishing of control. Just because Tom, Brian or David, a collaborator that is not a performer, is in the room, it [still] is a dictatorship. You don't get a say. If I say that's purple, it's purple. Someone might say 'Bryony actually that needs to be pink' and I will say 'no' or 'yes, good idea, great', but it's a dictatorship and there is something really control freaky about that. There is a vision that is unwavering to other artists. It's one artist. I hate collaborating with groups. It waters down any kind of essence for me. Solo work is one artist's vision and I think that I prefer that. I don't play well with others. I don't know what that means – probably that I'm a cunt.

MD: Maybe. But what about in the making though – if it was Bryony Kimmings Company do you think you would make things differently?

BK: When it's quite obviously a collaboration but we're still calling it a solo, there is something about reassurance and power that is really weird. I wouldn't be able to make this show without people telling me that I am right or that I am wrong. Someone is constantly scoring me and asking questions of me and without that I am nothing. That is really weird in a way because I assemble all these people around me, not because they agree with everything I say but because they ask difficult questions. I can't ask them of myself because my ego doesn't allow me – you can't see beyond your own tiny vision. So you assemble a team of provocateurs, and you have to keep saying, 'I have to do it that way because…' They are asking you questions, trying to make you see something and you have to go, 'I am doing it that way because I have said this before, and if I don't say it again then it's just once and it doesn't make sense'. They're doing it on purpose, that is what I am paying them for and it is a very strange pursuit. I will give you some money to come in and ask me if I'm doing the right thing all the time. It's weird but it's necessary and it's very un-egotistical to do that. I know that I can't make a decision about this. I am too emotionally involved or I think I am too good. Then there is also something really f****** weird about power. Wanting to be the director or the auteur. Wanting to have 'staff', to tell what to do. That is weird too. That is two really weird things about solo artists. It's kind of f***** up. I don't know why I just admitted that but sometimes you want to go 'no, go away and do this' coz you feel shit about yourself or whatever. I don't know, it's very strange.

MD: You are acknowledging the power that we all sometimes want, enjoy and play with. Some people talk about it, some people ignore it, some people deny it, some people pretend to be a democratic lover and really they are dictators.

BK: Maybe there's something about those people and the way in which they help create work that is infinitely testing you, so that you are ready when the curtains open and that first audience is there. With everybody asking you questions like, 'Why are you doing that? You look stupid when you do that. Do you know that you've already said that?', that is also what the audience will ask. There is a kind of logic to the self-flagellation of 'tear me to pieces every day, Tom, because I need rigorous testing like a car'. Then nobody in the press or the audience will say something that I haven't f****** considered. That is my paranoia. I had an early experience where I showed something too soon and the *Guardian* wrote about it and it nearly destroyed me. It was so embarrassing and from that moment on, I decided nothing gets past this gate without rigorous seatbelt testing.

MD: Also it's because you are alone in a devising situation. Again it is that simple thing that if you are working in a group making something, you are talking to each other, which you replicate solo using your dramaturg, Tom. In a group rehearsal, you get continual rehearsal feedback through conversation. And so finally, what haven't I asked you?

BK: I constantly ask myself 'Why do you think anyone cares? Who the f*** do you think you are?' That is something I have always struggled with. Part of me goes, 'because I am important and special', which is gross, and half of me goes, 'they don't and you're useless and there is no point in you doing it. Why are you even doing it?' I think that is a really intrinsic part of being a solo artist that you don't get when you are a collaborator. The constant doubt and the constant ego. Maybe that has not been asked: 'Why do you f****** bother?' That would be a rude question to ask someone though! … If you are an activist artist like I am or like you are, then your agenda is something you are constantly trying to hide. Which is weird because if you were a politician your agenda would be upfront.[21] You are constantly trying to trick people into considering your opinion or learning. Sometimes it's really nice when an artist just goes 'You know what? F****** blah blah blah blah'. Yeah, damn straight, but you have to earn the right to have a five-minute rant. I am thinking about Bobby Baker and how wonderful she is and her early work in the church. It's so good. Bobby Baker in a f****** church or someone pulling off a tablecloth and steam coming out. All of this talking and all of this thinking is to get to the simplest of things. One hour of the most perfect execution of an idea in the most simple way. It can take weeks to make a show and it's just an hour, and you think, 'God all that f****** work'. It is so stupid.

Endnotes

1. She collaborates with photographer Christa Holka and Alexander Innes (website and design) to create these images.
2. As I outline in the introduction to this book, I am including discussion of solo performance that are primarily the vision of one person and devised and performed by them although others may well be involved. I have therefore not included discussion of one of Kimmings' best-known pieces, *Credible, Likeable Superstar*, as it is clearly performed as a duet with Taylor, her 9-year-old niece. However, I have taken some liberties to include work that I think is interesting, while stretching my own boundary definitions, like her discussion of *Mega*, the audio-walk for one audience member wearing headphones who enacts the solo performance (Kimmings is not in it). I also include Kimmings' latest work, *Fake It Til You Make It*, where her partner, Tim, shares the performance space throughout, but where she holds the primary performance focus until the very end.
3. This 'knowing' is professional expertise in action – all these interviewees, as highly experienced practitioners, repeatedly reveal this ability.
4. Escalator Performing Arts promotes new performance and is based at The Junction, a theatre, gig and club venue in Cambridge, UK.
5. Stacey Makishi, describing herself as a 'transplant from Hawaii', also makes autobiographical work and is now a London-based associate artist with Chelsea Theatre and New Unity and produced by Artsadmin. See http://www.stacymakishi.com.
6. *7-Day Drunk* was commissioned by The Junction and Soho Theatre. It was created in June 2011 and toured the UK in 2011 and 2012 and Holland in 2013.
7. Mega is an audio-walk made for individual audience members who dress in pink shell suits, based on Kimmings' autobiographical narrative of the new burger restaurant, the Megatron, built on the side of the A14 outside Peterborough. It was created in March 2011, commissioned by The Junction and toured the UK.
8. *Mummy Time*, a variant on the one-to one performance genre (the audience is the fourth member of the family), was made in 2011 and performed in 2011 and 2012 at The Junction, Brighton Festival and Cruising for Art @ Vogue Fabrics in Dalston, London.
9. Again, this stretches the defining idea of 'solo' as there are several performers – however Kimmings played the lead performer initially and I included it as a compelling example of political one-to-one work which moves beyond this genre's often dominant aesthetics of purported intimacy and hush.

10. *Heartache, Heartbreak* was a piece initially made in a week for Culturgest, an arts festival in Lisbon, Portugal.

11. The Bush Theatre, in Hammersmith London, is renowned for staging new writing since 1972.

12. I have included in this interview the pieces *Mummy Time* and *Fake It Til You Make It* and elsewhere in this book discussion of work which has more than one performer in it, but only when the main performance focus still remains with the deviser–interviewee. Kimmings did talk about making her most well-known work to date – *Credible, Likeable Superstar Role Model*, which was informative in terms of how she devised with her 9-year-old niece. However, in performance the work was a duet, with both Kimmings and her niece, Taylor, drawing the audiences' focus. It is therefore not included in this interview.

13. 'Now' being October 2015, the time of interview.

14. Tim Grayburn is Kimmings' now ex-partner, a performer in *Fake It* and company member of Bryony Kimmings Ltd.

15. David Curtis-Ring is the designer for the majority of Kimmings' shows.

16. Krista Holka, photographer, and Alexander Innes (website and design).

17. Nina Steiger is a director and also works with Kimmings as her dramaturg.

18. Kimmings exemplifies here the solo artist as a devising writer, an authorship which does not first specify the words needed so much as the dynamic or action or event that needs to happen at that moment. In this, Kimmings can be aligned with other postdramatic theatre artists, who foreground the 'eventicity' of work – where scripted words are just a part of the narrative palette, alongside tone, music, dance or objects which also hold the meaning of the work.

19. Such a 'simplicity' derives, of course, from being able to use expert judgement, honed from experience over time. Expert artists are able to work at speed, as Kimmings evidences later on in the interview.

20. Choreographer Liz Lerman created the Critical Response Process, which offers a structured model through which an audience can give feedback. A good example of how it works can be found at https://vimeo.com/55022092.

21. For another comparison between the 'freedom' of politicians' routines compared to the restrictions on comedy routines, see Stewart Lee's discussion about the scrutinised, censored routines of comedians compared to the half truths allowed in politicians' speeches: http://www.theguardian.com/commentisfree/2015/oct/18/cameron-tell-lie-conservatives-conference-truth-decency-comedy-routines.

Tim Etchells

A Broadcast (2014) ©Tim Etchells

Tim Etchells is most widely known as the artistic director of the Sheffield-based theatre company Forced Entertainment, which he and other founder members started in 1984, after graduating out of Exeter University drama department in the UK. However, during the past twenty years, he has also expanded his own independent work in many directions, from solo theatre performances to video, visual art and installation projects in galleries and public spaces, as well as writing books, fiction and non-fiction. Etchells also collaborates regularly with other performance makers, both nationally and internationally.

Etchells speaks about four of his earlier solo performances in this interview: *Instructions for Forgetting* (2001), *Downtime* (2001), *In the Event* (2004) and *Words and Pictures* (2005). These mostly involve a performance lecture format, using spoken word, image and video. Solo working for Etchells is predominantly a contemplative, ideas-driven activity and space, and this is evident in how he speaks about his work. He is precise and detailed in how he makes work, which is hidden in the disarmingly casual performance aesthetic that characterises his solos. He is clearly experienced in being both 'inside' and 'outside' of the performance. Words like 'logics', 'economy', 'weight', 'perspective' and 'persona' occur frequently in this interview. His own participation as a 'character' in his work is framed as emerging from within the structure and requirements of each piece. He plays a disarming persona who starts 'low to the ground', so as to be able to delve into wild and weird places with his audiences. At the time of interview (2007), solo work was clearly a relatively 'new' area to discuss for a practitioner predominantly known for group theatre work. The interview provides evidence of his thinking as it unfolds, through conversation. Etchells is clearly able to apply his wide-ranging experience as a director and writer and his strong dramaturgical sensibility to our wider discussion of solo dramaturgy and his thinking incorporates numerous examples of other contemporary solo practitioners' work (Edit Kaldor, Eva Meyer-Keller, Walid Raad, Meg Stuart) as well as his own. Unsettling, shifting and layered – this describes the work as well as the interview.

Performance Chronology

Etchells' first solo, *Instructions for Forgetting* (2001), was made in collaboration with Hugo Glendinning (video) and Richard Lowdon (design). As with the later solos, it takes the form of a performance lecture, in which Etchells directly addresses the audience, speaking about the process of collecting the written and visual materials for the piece and showing video footage throughout. He moved away from the 'chatty narrator' style of delivery for his second piece, *Downtime* (2001), which involved a large-scale projection of his face onto a screen that he faces, speaking aloud his thought processes as the video unfolds. This performance was a twelve-minute piece, combining single-channel video and live performance. Later Etchells included the material from *Downtime* alongside several similar video and text fragments, which were organised together into a piece called *Words & Pictures* (2005). During this time, he also made *In the Event* (2004), another performance lecture using images by Hugo Glendinning, in which Etchells offers verbal portraits and remembered fragments from Forced Entertainment's (at that point) twenty-year history of collaborative performance making. In the presentation he reads from a written text but also uses the convention of 'footnotes' to mirror messy creative processes complete with diversions, disturbances and dead-ends. Etchells discusses this work as being constructed in a series of layers. *In the Event* includes reading the text described above and playing images of Forced Entertainment's work over the twenty-year period. It ends with Etchells' responses to three questions he sent to friends and colleagues, the final response being a playful list of people who might have replaced him in the performance. Since doing this interview, Etchells has also made two other solos for other performers – *Sight is the Sense that Dying People Tend to Lose First* (2008), performed by Jim Fletcher and *Although we fell short* (2011), performed by Kate McIntosh. His own solo work has also been expanded with the creation of a new performance using fragmented text and improvisation, titled *A Broadcast/ Looping Pieces* (2014).

Artist website: http://timetchells.com/

The Interview

MD: Can you tell me about how you make your solo work?

TE: The first solo was *Instructions for Forgetting*. The [making] process involved gathering material from other people. I had this idea that I would be on stage, which I am not normally, since I'm usually directing or writing text. My fantasy version of the project was about relinquishing control in some way – I thought I would just ask other people to send me videos and texts, and that I'd simply present the tapes and speak the text they'd sent. I wouldn't have to write anything, or do anything except to be there as a kind of conduit or mediator. That was the fantasy anyway! First I wrote to twenty or thirty people – friends or artists as well as family members – and said, 'Send me five minutes of video that you shot. It could be anything. You could have any reason for thinking that this was a good thing to send, and I may or may not use it in performance.' That was the initial idea.

I was thinking about the fact that I had a pile of videotapes which I had shot over the years, and that I'd never really looked at any of them. I was thinking, I know there are some nice things in there, and I was curious to see what other people might have and what they would send me. Then the tapes started to arrive. They were extremely diverse and puzzling, and I wasn't at all sure what I could do with them. I was tempted to intervene – writing my way into or around the material, but I resisted that. It was only then that it occurred to me that maybe the [next] best thing to do was to ask people for stories as well, stories not related to the tapes. So, responding to my second request people sent 'true stories' – whatever that meant to them. There was something in the juxtaposition of those stories and the tapes that seemed productive.

So making *Instructions* was about putting myself at the centre of a gathering process with the fantasy that I wouldn't have to write anything – I wanted it to be about the collecting and the arranging, not about my editorialising or adding material of my own. In the end though, I did have to intervene. Showing the work to people in the rehearsal process it was clear that I needed to be on the map somehow, in a more articulated way. I needed to be in the piece more substantially. Following this logic, it wasn't just about showing the tape that artist Franko B had given me, but about including the whole story of him giving me the tape and of me negotiating with him to get more of one particular segment of it. [In other words] the process of finding and selecting the material was [articulated] in the work.

MD: Can you remember how you discovered that?

TE: It rapidly became clear, as these totally random things arrived, that I couldn't find an easy way of making sense of it. The fact that it was a miscellany, that it all came from different people and different contexts, was important and needed to be brought out. It was pretty strategic to be honest: it was the only way to make sense of the material! People were sending me things with comments like 'Tim – I hope this is some use for the project' or 'don't know if this is the kind of thing you were thinking of but this happened to me a few years ago and that's when I made this recording'; or 'I like this because of the light…'; and I chose to include some of those simple framing texts from other people, to help locate the material. Again that seemed important. I could have done it differently – in rehearsal I certainly tried a blanker way of placing the videos and texts together in the piece, without context. But then things had a very mysterious or enigmatic presence and relationship to each other. You are thinking, 'Why the image of the dogs and at the same time a trip to Los Angeles? What is he trying to say?' Whereas, when I framed the material by talking about the process of collecting and about my relationship to the people, there was none of that irksome mystery at all. The fact that it didn't 'make sense' was excused to some extent and was lent a kind of coherence by the framing narrative of the process. The people writing to me to say they are going to give me something, and then me getting a video tape or an email a week or so later…, that became the story. So the piece has a poetics, but inside a fairly easy-going rational framework. I think that is how I work with other people. The attraction of the

Instructions for Forgetting (2001) ©Hugo Glendinning

simple set of rules and actions that causes the [performance] to be here – a simple process you can write on the back of a postcard – which then justifies or underwrites an awful lot of weirdness. Because the initial proposition is so straightforward, it is disarming.

Eventually I also wrote some material and put some tapes of my own into the mix – staying outside as 'just' a narrator–organiser of other people's material wasn't quite enough. The [main] principle of the project involves me as a gathering mechanism, inviting people to send something. That is quite a strong through line or interest for me in terms of how to make stuff alone – that structure of invitation. It's interesting because I guess it means that I am not really alone – I am subject to a lot of other influences, to the luck and happenstance of what I'm sent. But at the same time I am the person that is there to make sense of all the stuff that arrives … and I needed to be a little bit more in the mix in that role.

Having done *Instructions*, there was an urge to make a kind of sequel to it, and I conceived a number of similar kinds of projects where I planned to ask other people for different kinds of material. What I found, though, was that as I was developing ideas for an initial letter to send to people, I was already too knowing about the process I anticipated ahead. I was very aware of how I dealt with the random material in *Instructions* and before I'd even started making invites for the 'sequel' I found I was already constructing narratives and imagining framing texts. So even before the material for this notional second project had arrived, even before I had asked people for it, I was already predicting my response and how to deal with the project. Starting work on *Instructions*, I'd been totally naïve – making it up as I went along. But approaching the sequel, I was too pre- pared. I was worried about just treading the same path and that I'd be dealing with a very worked, self-conscious set of strategies. I just didn't really want to do it, and so I abandoned those plans.

So instead the next solo project – in 2000 – was a video piece that also found life as a live performance. In the process of creating the work I made a ten-minute recording of my face, while I was thinking about a particular topic. Then I made notes on what had gone through my mind and developed a commentary, in which I tried to describe what I had been thinking about during the ten minutes featured in the recording.

The text was a way of reading or narrating the changes of my expression, and the shifts of focus; the moments where I laughed or looked sad and so on. Based on my notes, I really tried to give a narrative account of what had gone through my mind. Of course, that is a kind of preposterous process – condensing the abstract, meandering of thought into language. Thought is so much more speedy, so much more elusive. So in the act of translation between the two what you end up with is a kind of fiction. But it was a fiction that genuinely tried to reconstruct, or refer to, what had gone through my mind in the time of the recording, in so far as that was possible. The short performance made in this way was called *Downtime* and I presented it live as part of a double bill with the choreographer and dancer Meg Stuart.[1]

Over the years, since 2000, I occasionally made more of these recorded 'thinking pieces', in which I again thought about a particular topic and then made notes on the thinking and tried to re-construct it as a kind of spoken narrative. I took a bunch of these and put them together to make a new solo performance called *Words & Pictures* that lasts an hour and ten minutes. It comprises projection of seven of these tapes, one after another, with live commentary where I am trying to reconstruct what I thought.[2] In some ways it is the exact opposite of the process on *Instructions* where I was asking for material from other people. There is nobody else in *Words & Pictures*. It is me, looking at my own face, describing myself, re-telling my own thoughts. In the performance I don't turn around much because I have to face the screen. It's a big projection, but I can't have a direct contact with the audience because I am so busy trying to keep track of where a certain blink is on the projected recording, or where a certain smile is, in order to say the right thing.

MD: What do you mean when you say 'the right thing'?

TE: For each recording I have notes – effectively a script and a list of time codes relating to feature moments on the tape – so that I can keep track of where things are and where I need to be in the narration of my thoughts. With *Down Time*, the first recording I worked on in 2000, I know the material well enough to do the performance without anything written down. With the more recent recordings, I needed notes to help me navigate and make sense of what was there. *Words & Pictures* is really the opposite [of *Instructions*] in a way, because it is an incredibly circular act of digging deep. It's not hugely confessional! But it does feel rather private and contemplative. Whereas *Instructions* the other solo is much more (pause) 'social'. A strange word for a solo – but these two pieces are in some ways perhaps at the opposite ends of what is possible.

MD: So that brings up the question of the role of your self in your solo work – showing yourself or not…

TE: Yeah – I think for me it starts in the writing I have done around performance. From quite early on, with Forced Entertainment [FE], I set about writing on the work and the process and ideas around it. As part of that I developed a personal way of writing that included anecdote and kinds of autobiographical material – an 'I' and a set of fictional 'I's, versions of myself, and of other people in the company. Increasingly, I thought of that writing in performative terms – in the way that it built relations with readers, opened spaces, constructed journeys. I mean, at some level I don't see much difference between writing an essay or a text for a conference and writing or making what we might call a performance piece. Things unfold in time or they unfold on the page. They unfold in a theatre or they unfold in a lecture theatre or they unfold on screen. But it's all dramaturgy; it's all about creating a presence and subverting it, about opening a space of ideas and then suddenly focusing attention in a certain way. You can think of these things as they might happen on a stage, but I think of a page as much the same thing. It's another frame. Several of the texts in which I had written about FE's work, or about ideas surrounding that work, were already rather [like] 'solo performances'. They used autobiographical material, and were very much predicated on staging an 'I' in relation to the other kinds [of] material. *Instructions for Forgetting* was really the first proper 'solo performance' that I made and it drew on strategies I'd already touched on in those other kinds of written texts – it was a chance to go a bit further with that.

MD: So an aspect of yourself is there – you are playing with the representation of yourself in the work in different ways.

TE: Yes. It's there in the critical writing.[3] And, in theatre terms, there has always been an interest for me as a director in the moment where the silly costume comes off at a certain point, and the question of who's left standing there? The actor beyond or under 'role', without costume. What are we left looking at? Who is underneath? Even if you think about the Forced Entertainment piece *First Night*,[4] the smile that the performers sport through much of the performance is a kind of mask. There is a kind of assumption of character and fiction in that mask, and when it drops at certain moments you just see the person stood there... I am very fascinated with that kind of transition, and with the sudden appearance of 'the real person' under the task. That idea of realness (problematic of course) is pretty strong in the work. I think the solo work has pulled me even closer to that idea of underneath... of a self that emerges from under or between other things.

MD: In solo work, something you always also have to deal with is being accused of narcissism, the 'what is so interesting about you?' question. It's often a kind of mis-reading of what is going on, but it happens a lot. We have that image of you on video thinking and you on stage, telling us about you... someone might come along and say – 'so what?'

TE: Yes. I do see that as something you have to cover your back on. I think in *Instructions*, that was easy to do because the basic frame of it was outward looking – I was asking other people for materials. I guess if you wanted to be horrible, you could say that it was 'an exhibition of Tim Etchells and interesting people that have written to him'. But at least it gave weight to things that people sent to me, and you can see some kind of risk and generosity in my giving that space to others and the images or narratives they sent to me. So I think some of the 'me-ness' is deflected into, or refracted into, all these other people who contributed to the project. The other work, *Downtime/Words & Pictures*, is perhaps tougher to defend on that score in the sense that it really is just me, looking at versions of me. For that reason, I think it is probably a less successful piece!

MD: It reminds me of a brilliant Vietnamese filmmaker and writer called Trinh T Minh Ha, do you know her work? She writes very eloquently about the difference between offering a kind of 'me-ness' and the notion of 'the multiple I' – the first in danger of falling into a kind of narcissism, the other a much more generative, connected way of dealing with self. It seems to me you are very much engaged with exploring this connected, multiple self. Your presence, for example, on stage is both as a casual being and yet clearly you are dealing with a lot of material and timing and specific texts – you are performing in a very considered way.

TE: Yeah. I think [in *Instructions*] I am trying to just be there and establish this everyday quite ordinary thing, though there is another level to that always of course. I think about it as the establishment of a bottom line – making a place from which you can move on. In *Instructions* there is an attempt to be friendly basically – not very arty and not very intellectual – a bit blokeish I think. Then, having established that mode, the persona and the piece can become a bit more complex and thoughtful. It's quite common in a lot of work that I have done that it tries to come in quite low to the ground. It feels banal in a certain way and from that banality it has permission, or ambition, to go to other places. A degree of ordinariness – it's disarming.

MD: Yes, it is disarming, that deliberate everydayness that is set up. I just wonder what that does. Sometimes as an audience member I find that much less disarming than someone coming on and doing a great leap. You know where you are in that world. Whether it interests one or not, virtuoso displays are very relaxing, because it is what it is – nothing is going to jump out at you. Whereas with your work, it sets up a real tension and yet it is also saying 'relax'.

TE: I can see that. It is contrived and strategized… What's interesting perhaps is that while it is very deliberate in that sense the relationship to the audience in a work like *Instructions* also has a pretty close and straightforward relation to what is actually happening, to actual reality. I'm there, I know you're there. I'm going to read from the papers in front of me… sometimes I'll need a drink of water… it's 'simple'!

MD: Moving on, are there any other pieces we have not discussed?

TE: Those two are the main ones but there are some other, smaller things that might be relevant. The first is a solo called *In the Event*, a kind of a halfway house between lecture and performance I made in 2004–2005. The basis is a kind of essay-cum lecture text with many footnotes that looks back over what was then the twenty years of FE's work. This core text has a prelude and a postscript in which I'm answering a series of questions people sent to me following an invitation to contribute to the project – so related to *Instructions*, in that sense… There's also a middle section – a five-minute interlude with music and projected images of the company from the previous twenty years.

The beginning is quite informal, not fully scripted, in which I am answering questions that people have sent me. I was drawing on a previous project (a lecture in Frankfurt) where I used this device – asking for questions, and then opening them, previously unseen, responding to them live as part of the performance. There were a few questions that came up from the Frankfurt thing that were very productive, so I start *In The Event* by going back to two of them, and I close the piece by going back to a third. The final question is 'In the event that you weren't here tonight, doing this, who would/should or could be?' and in answer I give a long list of people who I think it might be somehow apt – good or funny or important – if they were there rather than me – other artists and writers, performers, friends, family members. It's a way of filling the room somehow, with other possible narratives and perspectives. So the piece sandwiches this rather anecdotal material at the beginning and end with the dense poetic footnotes text in the middle and a further island of images and music nested within that. The relation between textual information – filling people's minds with stuff – and, by contrast, the act of creating space, is really important to me. It's about putting certain ideas in the air, then creating space in which they can be dealt with privately; letting people drift or free-associate or go off in different directions.

MD: Is that your aim, in making solo work?

TE: Yes, for me the solo thing has been a way to deal a little bit more explicitly with ideas, with thinking. That's why it links back to writing about the work. By contrast the theatre work I have done with Forced Entertainment has tended to work much more through action and image, often in playful or illogical combinations of things. I think the solo work has tended to be more ideas driven, creating a more contemplative space. It becomes a space in which to reflect, about the work and about the world. So in *Instructions for Forgetting*, there is material about the idea of 'rehearsing' – about rehearsing for performance, but also about the way that people in their own lives prepare or rehearse for certain things. So for me it's talking about the world and about ideas in a slightly different way than I can in 'proper' theatre work (laughs).

MD: That is interesting because I was talking to someone last night about solo work who was saying 'I don't ever think of seeing solo work as seeing solo work'.

TE: Yes.

MD: Perhaps what you were talking about then was that writing and thinking and reflecting are different things from 'proper theatre'.

TE: Sure. I mean it is not a distinction I *really* believe in, but there is part of me that separates 'proper' fully theatrical shows with costumes and music and so on, from 'improper' shows that might involve sitting down at a table, talking a lot and thinking. It's a pragmatic distinction, a way of thinking about work in different modes and understanding the economies they operate in; and both of those modes are important to me.

MD: Especially in relation to you because you are a writer and as you say, all along your practice has been one of writing. You are doing a talking practice to me now and your main practice is a writing practice and a directing practice and I wonder if it is a problem that I am getting people to do a practice that is not their primary practice.

TE: Talking?

MD: Yes. Talking about making work. You are used to writing about the work, so you are fluent in thinking about it, whereas some people might not be, because in fact they just do it.

TE: Yeah I think that is really interesting, but then all artists have a talking practice somehow don't they? Even 'well I don't really know' is a way of talking about what you do! We all develop strategies. I just did some interviews about a project I made with a group of children and young people in Belgium,[5] and the first few interviews I did about the piece were really weird because of course I hadn't really talked about it before in that particular public way. So in the interviews I was really thinking, really trying to figure out what to say – finding appropriate language, thinking it through. Once you have done a few [interviews], you figure out a line, and figure out what people want or need to hear and as a practice it becomes more contained, whereas at the very beginning you often don't really know what to say about a work – the language isn't there right away. It needs work. But in the end every artist has to find a position, a way to narrate or talk about what they do. Even saying 'I don't like talking, I just do things,' is a kind of decision on how to talk.

MD: There is a gap.

TE: Yeah – you can try to close that gap between the work and your articulation of it to some extent or try to be more true to what you do, but making things in the studio is unmappable so far as I'm concerned; complicated and concrete in ways that mean any kind of reflection on the process or the work itself is always going to be a distortion. The work and the language around it are not the same thing. Normally for me, my understanding of what I am doing lags behind the work itself by some distance. It often feels easier to talk about stuff I did three years ago than it might be to speak about what I am doing now. Because at best the work itself, the current work, is slightly outside of my established frameworks, my known patterns. I mean the current practice is slightly out of reach of the discourse. I don't see a problem with that, it's just a fact that there are gaps between those things.

MD: What other devising strategies do you use for making solo work?

TE: I think this device of asking people for things is quite strong for me. I also used it in this choir project *Safety Measures*, for which I asked people to send me stories about songs that they use to protect themselves in certain ways.[6] Or asking people for questions, as I did for the Frankfurt thing I mentioned, or asking them for stories and tapes in *Instructions*. What I am probably looking to do is to be subject to the decisions of other people. Because in a way, that is a foil to being unbearably alone, and unbearably in control. The great thing about somebody sending you very specific material is that you have to deal with it. The piece has to find a way to negotiate this entirely different bit [of] territory or narrative that you didn't think of. You had no idea that that narrative or idea was going to arrive in the post or email that morning. The out-of-controlness of that is really lovely.

MD: This is a bizarre thing, that as a solo practitioner I might decide to do something solo and somewhere in me there must be a belief in it, and yet then I find lots of strategies for not being alone, or of not being in control.

TE: Yes – maybe you have to do that when you are working alone. Working with the company or in other collaborations there are already other people in the room and they are always already doing something other than what I might have anticipated. Gathering is one [mechanism for dealing with that issue] and the other mechanism is what I'd think of as subjection to a rule. In *Instructions* the rule was making a performance using donated material. I had some leeway, allowing me to rewrite or edit texts for example, but fundamentally I was committed to making the performance with what people sent me. That was my rule and I was rather trapped in it; not free anymore but rather constrained in something, subject to self-imposed limits and the will of others. In one sense it's very free to work alone, but perhaps what one is trying to do is within that freedom is to make limits – to limit your freedom, otherwise it is meaningless.

MD: Without ultimately trapping yourself into something that is too tight.

TE: Absolutely. In making *Words and Pictures*, there was also a rule about everything being done via the video tapes, and the act or process of my narrating my thought process. All of the sections of the pieces were made under task conditions: the camera is set up, I decide what I am going to think about, I think, I make the notes on what I thought. So again I am subject to accidents or bits of chance. I am subjugated to the circumstances and specificities of what happens when the camera is running and I am therefore rather out of control, having agreed to do this. Having decided that narrating the video tapes is a good idea, I then have to live with the consequences; articulating myself through what is essentially a quite limiting form. But in a way, accepting a set of limitations is saving yourself from gratuitousness: the state of 'I can do anything' is horrible!

MD: Like total freedom in improvisation can be crippling.

TE: Yes. So in terms of overall strategies; subjecting oneself to input from others, setting limits, setting frames, rules and structures – devices or modes that contain but also make fertile a certain area of enquiry or activity – that would all seem quite key to working solo.

MD: What do you then do, to further develop the work?

Words and Pictures (2005) ©Hugo Glendinning

TE: I tend to think of each performance in terms of its game or economy – the system or systems through which it works. Developing the work, in one sense, is about discovering the edges of those games or economies, finding out what might be the extreme moves or possibilities for expression inside them. So in *Words and Pictures*, it was clear that I had a lot to say in narrating some of the video tapes and less to say in relation to others – there was a variable, a dynamic in the amount of information provided in each case. Realising this I had the idea that there should be one videotape about which I would have absolutely nothing to say – where I would claim to have lost the notes or where I might say that I didn't want to reveal what I was thinking about. Identifying what the possible extremes of a game or task are is always quite an important part of the process for me. It's a matter of figuring out what the pleasures of the mode or material might be and figuring out what the punches of it might be. Ron Vawter from the Wooster Group said a nice thing to me[7] – that they spend a lot of time in their process 'juggling the material' and getting to know the different weights of it and that then at a certain point, armed with that knowledge they are ready to make the piece, ready to make a composition from the materials. With my *Instructions* performance, as material came in, I was sifting and processing it in that kind of way – trying to understand it. Once I identified things that worked for me I was able to look for or otherwise create more of the same – rewriting or shifting its weight to another place by editing. So that is one process of how to move on – figuring out what the economy of the work is, what the extremes of it are, what its pleasures are, what its pains are; working out the weight and possibilities of the things you are dealing with. Another part of the process for me is starting to put things in sequence, seeing how things I have collected or made can sit next to each other – what they do to each other, how they interact? That is also a really important part of figuring out what the dynamic economy of a work is.

MD: Do you do that in writing or visually?

TE: By doing, really.

MD: I guess if it is video you edit it together.

TE: Yeah, by putting it together or if it's performance stuff, by writing or reading or doing it – reading the texts, putting things in sequence, seeing how they feel. In the case of *Instructions*, where people were sending in stories and video tapes, I would just read different bits of the material in sequence, one after another, to see what that felt like. And then I'd put it all in another sequence, and read it all again. You get to know something by doing that; putting it into time and space rather than just looking at the materials on the page. You can learn something from looking at materials on the page for sure, but if it is text, I think you learn more [by] reading it out or by doing it.

MD: Particularly with your body, I think. With *Words and Pictures*, I am interested in what your body is doing there and of course you need to be doing it to see what happens.

TE: Yes.

MD: Otherwise you could just be a voice, couldn't you?

TE: Yes, and I think with all of those things, how you as a physical body can negotiate being there and how you are saying something – whether it is comfortable to be saying that kind of thing – these are all things that you can not necessarily know while sitting at a computer. It is much easier to figure that kind of stuff out if you are actually in a space and trying it out, realising that this might be a bit awkward. In *Instructions*, I did a lot of editing of the texts, but I had to read stuff out in order to realise that various people's flowery descriptions were better remade as simpler or starker – it works much better that way in performance terms. It's fine as writing, but testing things against a live process...

Instructions for Forgetting (2001) ©Hugo Glendinning

MD: The live situation is doing something, and it's finding out what that situation is doing.

TE: Yes, absolutely. What is this bloke doing here? What's his relationship to audience? What's the dynamic? I generally want to get on to doing this kind of stuff as soon as possible – even if I'm putting material on the stage in the most crude, rubbish way, [be]cause you learn so much and the piece can then grow around your doing it.

MD: The statement you made earlier – about it all being about dramaturgy – creating presence, subverting, opening space and focusing – I find it a useful possible summary of what you do in your making.

TE: I think it is very much what we were talking about. What is the initial register or mode of the performance, what is the initial contract, what is the initial framework or expectation or negotiation that you establish with the viewer? And having ... established that initial mode, what are the ways you can push, manipulate or twist it? And I think that is the same in a performance, as it is in a novel, or in a bit of music. Not that I have written any music! But basically it's about time and about structure. So I do see those things as being pretty equivalent. I suppose what is interesting is that fundamentally it's this 'post dramatic thing' – where the drama moves to being a drama about the relation with the audience, rather than being a drama about the people on stage.[8] I am very interested in that.

MD: In what?

TE: In this question of the evolving dynamic relation between the spectator and the work; in the way that the work wants to create heat, or intimacy, in the way that these states or experiences get negotiated in public. Because that is what is happening in the theatre; that is what it is, as a form, more than anything else.

For me in these solo works, there's a conscious manipulation of the relationship with the audience, often around questions of trust or 'likeability' for example. In the early parts of *Instructions* I set up a straightforward, pretty genial presence only to subvert and challenge that as the piece goes on. There's a whole chunk of the performance which re-tells a story about a visit to the cinema with my son – his first visit to the cinema, which was quite traumatic. I always perform the latter part of this narrative rather harshly and hard and I can feel people in the audience going like [he mimes moving backwards]… Just being able to twist the material and the relation to them in this kind of way is really important. It's what the piece is built from really – these shifts of mode or voice, shifts in people's understanding. Sometimes the piece enters a more poetic space – like a section of endless mutating George Best anecdotes, or a letter from a friend who describes a family friend who's in prison – these again have a very different register and they paint me as narrator in a different light through the content but also through the way I am reading them. It's like once a starting point for my presence or persona is established, what are the possibilities for moving it around and doing different things with it? And the question of if the audience 'like' or trust or care about the version of me on the stage really becomes a topic. I think that's often true in terms of solo work. The likeable and not likeable – that thing is quite high in the mix.

MD: It can be, although not everyone chooses to say that that is the topic.

TE: I think it's a dynamic whether it's spoken of or not – the relation to the person you are watching, your understanding of them, your reading of them, your trust of them, the extent to which you might like, desire, question, doubt or be fascinated by or interested in them. I guess another way to think about this structure of change and development in the relationship between performer and audience is to say that in performance you expect that things will get more complicated and more interesting as time goes along. It doesn't matter where you start but after twenty minutes people need to feel like they are in a slightly different place. And again after forty minutes they need to feel they are in a slightly different place again. And again after sixty minutes and so on. There has to be a thickening, or a process whereby we go further or deeper, or whereby things become more complex. Stasis is not really an option. Even work that ostensibly pursues an idea of stasis is not really static; if we imagine a performance that repeats the same thing again and again we know that over time the thing changes and our response to it changes. So if you think about repetition in half an hour of Jan Fabre or Pina Bausch or John Cage, we know that the same actions repeated [are] simply not the same at all. But we expect thickening, we expect opening. In *Instructions* I can start with 'Mr Genial Chatty Bloke', but people would be very bored if I was still doing that after half an hour. Things need to change.

MD: Returning to those words: creating a presence, subverting it, opening a space, focusing in ... what is the focusing in?

TE: It's just dramaturgy really. In the set up for many shows, in the first half hour or so, maybe longer, anything might be possible – we enjoy the fact that lots of ideas or themes might be circulating, that energy can be going in different directions, that things are thrown up in the air. As an economy that's establishing itself, setting out some ground rules, that's definitely fine for a while, but unless the work narrows and confirms its interest in one thing or another, again, it is not very interesting. It's a matter of time and structure. Dramaturgy – that narrowing or focusing produces the sense for audience that we are getting closer to the point of this. You do rather want that, as a watcher; it's connected to the idea of thickening that I was speaking of earlier. In narrative theatre that might be framed through plot and character development but in the kind of work I'm interested in it's often rather more abstract. You can't just keep throwing balls in the air.

MD: Yes. Like one of the real dangers of improvisation is that you just keep creating new things.

TE: Yes, and it's very, very boring isn't it? One of the things that I often say about dramaturgy, and it relates strongly to IFF, is the idea of 'live by the sword, die by the sword'. So if you set up the frame of the piece asking friends for video tapes and stories, then you have to make the show work through that device – you have to follow through. It's hard to do something that's half an hour of that and then half an hour later divert to some other tactic. There's a demand to be consequent – to follow and fully exploit the frames you put in place. I saw a really interesting piece – *Blessed* (2007) by Meg Stuart – in Brussels last year; a solo with one dancer in a space made of cardboard and into which it rains constantly. As the time goes on in the piece, the entire set collapses and becomes sodden and the performer in this environment becomes very pathetic, soaked, slipping around. It's a great example of a very singular idea taken right to the limit and it works really well. But towards the end of the piece two new performers arrive, each of whom makes a five-minute intervention in the performance. It was pretty hard to develop an interest in these new people that close to the end of the work, you have no stake in them. Once you have so clearly established an economy, it's quite hard to break it by bringing on the cavalry from the wings.

MD: In the making process, is there a point at which, once you try out some sequencing and you are in the space doing it, you might get someone in?

TE: Yes – often I will have people come by and watch and make comments and say 'oh yeah I was engaged by that', or 'I was bored there', or 'I have got a big problem with the whole thing, this really needs to be addressed, what are you doing?' Those kind of questions! Generally when working either with the group, or on my own, I like people to come by and watch.

MD: People? You are someone who likes several people to see it?

TE: Yes. There are people in the company, who, if I am working on my own, I would definitely invite, but also if anybody was in the neighbourhood who fancied coming by. For example, when we were finishing *Instructions for Forgetting* in Vienna, there were a whole bunch of artists in the festival and several people came by, even those I didn't know necessarily, who watched rehearsals and made comments.

MD: And you don't find that confusing?

TE: Not really, no. Generally I find it very useful and I'm more or less able to sift or interpret people's comments in constructive ways. I guess I generally use them to confirm or deny my own suspicions.

MD: So who else do you collaborate with to make solo work?

TE: It has varied a bit. In *Instructions* I had Richard [Lowdon] from FE on stage operating all the video, so he was there through a lot of the making process and Hugo Glendinning, the photographer, also worked on the video material, editing and sticking it together, so he was in and out quite a lot. A lot of the process was me sitting at home with all the stuff that people had sent me. Writing and trying combinations and stuff like that. So in that one, there were two people quite formally with me while I was making it. They were both feeding into all aspects of the project effectively, because they were there all the time, and I also wanted to know what they thought about things – the sequence of material or the narrative, the performance mode and so on. The other solos, *In The Event* or *Words and Pictures*, those were made much more privately. I just did them, really. I think a couple of times people stopped by and watched run throughs or maybe I asked them for advice on very specific questions: 'Do you think I should do this or this?' I find that interesting actually. I have it a bit with my girlfriend who's also an artist – she lives in New York and I will often send her a bunch of stuff on email or as video to look at to help me make a decision. It's liberating to let someone else decide. To take some aspect of it out of your own hands.

MD: Your voice changes when you talk about *Words and Pictures* and *Instructions for Forgetting* – they are really different works, aren't they?

TE: I think when I was talking about *Instructions* as a bit of a 'show show' – I don't think I am really that interested to make 'show shows', with me in them. So I think I am gravitating more towards the things that sit more towards lecture-performance, or don't quite sit inside something you would put on in a theatre and sell tickets for.

MD: Why? What is the difference? What if I said, 'Tim I don't see a difference between a "show show" and a show'?

TE: Perhaps it is more a mental distinction I use, again to do with how different works negotiate theatre and the expectations that go with theatre. Because a lot of the work I've done, with the group or solo, is about negotiating the problem of theatre – audiences and expectations. The more of a show show it is the more it feels it has to grapple with all that, and the less of a show show it is the more those concerns and questions don't seem to matter. As if being somehow under the theatrical bar, outside the category almost, allows a certain liberation. Most likely this is just a way of conning myself – that if what I'm making is not exactly a 'show' I have permission to do something different. I guess I want that because I spend most of my performance-making time working on pieces that really operate as 'shows' and have to deal with that whole tyrannous economy of theatre.

MD: You are talking about the work with FE.

TE: Yes. I like the solo work to be in a space where I don't have to think about those same questions. I think a lot of the desire to be oneself, to just 'be there as a person', to deal with ideas in a relatively straightforward way, to not be involved in a hugely complicated, theatrical process – those are all means of staging an escape. [It's] about getting out of the thing I spend most of my working time doing. Looking at it in this way the fact that I would want to keep the solo stuff on the minimal edge of performance makes some sense to me. Do you know what I am saying? There is an interesting contrast between *Instructions* and *Words and Pictures*; *Instructions* is on the more theatrical edge, quite generous and here for you, whilst in *Words and Pictures* I am looking at the screen all the time.

MD: I was interested by you having your back to us.

TE: It's a refusal, in a way.

MD: It ties in with the notion of being in the shadow – I was talking with Terry last night about wanting to be a shadow puppet.

TE: Yes, the persona in *Instructions* is forwards and friendly and charming as far as I can manage that, and I didn't really want to stay in that mode for another piece. I don't want to be Spalding Gray, monologuing, sitting behind a table, that storytelling thing, which is great of course but it felt like a smart move for me to step away from that and go to a different place.

MD: You have talked about why you work solo or how that relates to your other work and the positive sides in that. Are there also problems for you, working solo?

TE: I'd say the problems are bound up with the positive things. It's great that you can just get on with it and that not everything has to be discussed. You can work intuitively, let things circulate in your own head without pinning them down into words, or decisions, or an argument.

You can let something process on the back burner, in the way that things do. When I'm working with other people, at least in FE, everything gets put into words and we spend a lot of time talking together and criticising what we did in rehearsals. Working solo, of course I do that in my own head, but it's not quite such a tortuous process. I guess the pitfall though is precisely that working solo, things aren't subjected to that kind of collective scrutiny.

It's certainly more peaceful working on my own, more peaceful and things take their own time a bit more. I'd say that as a group at FE we are quite good at letting things drift and take time, but there is still the pressure of the critical conversations that you have to have. Whereas in a way, when you are working on your own, you can be free of those, to a certain extent at least. I'd see that as the advantage and the problem.

MD: You can do it anywhere, can't you? When you have your laptop you have your home with you. I write as well, and there is something about solo not being a million miles away from some sort of writing practice.

TE: Yes. The thing it associates to most closely for me is working on fiction, and that's probably the work I like doing better than anything else. I feel very connected then and very centred, where working with the group is always a quite fractious experience. I mean it's been 24 years of it,[9] so it can't be that bad! But it is hard. I do like to have a way of working that is to do with solo and to do with text and I can just be in the space of the work more privately.

MD: Can you describe a favourite moment from a solo you have made or seen?

TE: There is a moment in Edit Kaldor's *Or Press Escape* where she has been on a computer, writing out emails and filling out forms on the internet and doing various things. You have been watching her through the medium of what is projected on the screen. You don't see her face in the performance. She is busy with the computer. You just get to know her and the story that you are engaged in through what is projected, which is the screen of the computer she is working on. And then at a certain moment in the performance as she is working she gets a message from the computer to say that the hard drive is full and that she needs to clear some space. It's a deliberate thing, an event she has manufactured in the dramaturgy of the work, and programmed into the computer. But in response she embarks on a process of tidying the computer desktop; putting things in folders and throwing away various files. In this five-minute section she takes it from a super messy desktop to one that's incredibly organised. And in the process of the tidying she opens a lot of movie files and plays them and trashes them and then opens the trash again and decides to save one of them. You basically see her weighing up all this material and while she does it, there is music. It's basically five minutes of watching somebody organise material on their computer, but I guess what has happened in the previous forty-five minutes is that you've built up enough narrative and other kinds of information about her that this act is able to make sense. It also a moment of space – you've been filled with stuff: textual information and images and dilemmas and ideas and then suddenly you get this lovely five minutes of looking at a big screen and watching these things go into folders. There are no words anymore, it is just the organisation of this material on the desktop and that is really great. You can think and make what you can of what is happening, and it is done at exactly the right moment in the piece, dramaturgically. You are just ready to be let go, and it works really really well.

And then a moment from a performance by Eva Meyer-Keller, a solo artist whose amazing performance *Death is Certain* involves her enacting deaths on forty cherries. The piece takes place in a room, with the audience standing, gathered around. She has two tables, one empty and one laid out with lots [of] materials: a razor blade, matches, string, a cheese grater, a toy car and on and on – as well as forty cherries. The moment I am thinking of takes in the first couple of 'deaths' she enacts. She picks up one of the cherries and takes it to the second table, the empty one. She also takes the string and some sellotape. She brusquely ties one end of the string around the stalk of the cherry, tapes the other to the table and then lets the cherry drop so that it hangs there from the edge of the table. Done. Then she goes back to the first table and comes back with a razor blade and another cherry. Once there she uses the blade to slowly peel all the skin off the cherry, puts it down, done. Then she goes to get another one.

She gives no opinion at all about what she is doing. Her performance mode is somewhere between cookery demonstration and TV science presenter, with a hint of death camp technician. It's very blank. She is not telling you anything – not robotic, just doing what she is doing. I think in both of these examples what I am absolutely drawn to is the space – there is room for you as a spectator. There is a need, an invitation for you to project, to fill space with meaning. I suppose what is interesting about that is that as artists they have done something, they have made a proposition in and to the room. But there is also a kind of refusal, in the blankness I am speaking of, which means that as a viewer, you are forced to be very active. Perhaps this is something of a counter to this question of narcissism we were talking about before – in that this is solo work that nonetheless manages to open a space for other people. I find that so productive.

Thinking about that idea, and that sense of blankness, makes me think about *Instructions*, and the blank video tape I describe being sent as a contribution to the piece and that I say [I] want to show in the performance. Showing a part of that tape functions as a kind of short interval, a pause in the regular business of the piece. We have been looking at images and hearing stories so thick and fast to that point in the show that somehow it pays to have this 'nothing', this twenty seconds of blank tape. Of course you think 'What is that?' and 'Why would someone send that?' And at the same time it's just dead simple; it makes you look at the blank screen with the static on it and, seeing that, spending time with that makes you see images differently. You are awakened to the possibility of no image and at the same time you get to re-see the images themselves. I'm thinking of those Warhol screenprints in pairs – the *Electric Chair* ones, and others – where he put a screen-printed image on one side and a monochrome screen-print canvas on the other. Your eye is constantly going from one side to the other. The space of the second canvas is a kind of blank – it serves as a screen for your projections, a negation of the narrative in the other canvas.

I think in *Instructions* the dance piece for me at the end works in a related way – as a kind of blank space. It is probably one of the first times in the piece that there is little talking. There is doing – action, choreography – traffic noise and music. We are towards the end of the piece. There is no language content. It becomes a reflective space in which what we have heard and talked about in the previous one hour and twenty minutes is allowed to circulate, privately, for people. And then it's cut.

MD: There is a confidence in that. Like holding a stillness so other people can move. When I think of a solo, *Taj A Chino Blues*, that I made in 2006, I was too nice, I gave too much. I was trying to use niceness as a mode, as a strategy because I was talking about racial politics, overt politics, but still I couldn't seem to help myself doing too much.

TE: Do you know Walid Raad's work? He is a Lebanese artist living in New York. He has done several lecture performances. He saw *Instructions* in Vienna and said he was going to borrow two small things from the piece – he was interested in the way that I was onstage as people were coming in, and in the way that I had a pen with my text, to make notes as I went along! He spoke about these as being very fundamental 'grounding' moves in the piece – things that underscore the very immediate 'presentness' of what I'm doing and its relation to the audience. He works a similar space – very much real time, lecture mode, but there is also something very mischievous and sometimes completely confounding about what he is doing. His on-going project is called The Atlas Group, which he describes as 'studying and collecting real and fictitious documents from the Lebanese wars'. In the lecture works he shows these documents, which are often quite outrageously weird, and which he explains through various narratives. In the discussions he sets up after the presentations, people in the audience often question if what he is showing them is real or not and he always comes back with a statement that the Atlas group 'collects and manufactures documents'. It's a denial and a confirmation at the same time (laughter). He works this super charming friendly persona, but also insists on this confounding position between documentary and fiction – so you can never quite trust the charm, there's something unsettling in the air also. What I love is that in the discussions he always manages, in every reply, to re-assert the problem that people's questions have flagged.

MD: If I say the word 'solo', what does that conjure up for you?

TE: I suppose two things. One – a certain kind of fragility or vulnerability, as we discussed. Like you showed up without your mates to stick up for you – a basic aloneness, in front of the audience. And related to that, I suppose I think about how the lone person on-stage doesn't have a nexus of other forces acting on them to cause change, or provoke new action in what they are doing. Often in the other work I do, with the group, what causes change on stage is the dynamic negotiation between different people with different intentions and understandings of what's going on. Conflict, adaptation, change – when you are on your own, a lone figure on the stage, there is no one else to knock you off course. So you have to invent other ways.

MD: It brings up the theme of being in control or being out of control. So different people will, as you say, set up conditions... Mike [Pearson], for example, in his piece *Bubbling Tom* is a tour guide around his village and he has got huge amounts of text to get through, that he has learnt. And then what happens is, because he knows all these people and he is very close to them spatially, they interrupt him all the time. And on the one hand he just deals with that, but on the other he hadn't expected it, even though he had set it up. He was surprised when he first did it that people felt that they could interrupt him so easily and gossip with him and yet he had completely set the whole thing up like that. And of course in some ways that is interesting in terms of what solo people do, either consciously or not, to create dynamic.

TE: Yes, quite. It's the problem, isn't it? I suppose one person acting in a vacuum of their own will or intention – that is likely to be quite boring. So you have to find ways that they encounter some kinds of structure, or impetuses, or forces from outside. I suppose, to be honest, if you are a dancer and you decide to dance to Bach or Janis Joplin then you are already in a kind of dialogue or negotiation with that other work, aren't you? Bach is a kind of limit and restriction and a thing you are forced to deal with; what you want to do has to negotiate with what Bach already did. So music is an easy one. In *Instructions*, I am basically entering into a dialogue with the desires of other people – the materials they have sent me as text and video – in order to not sit there and just be telling about what Tim Etchells knows and thinks – which would be very boring!

MD: Although in a way that is what you exactly do in *Words and Pictures*.

TE: Yeah, that piece is wrapped around itself in that way. Although the problem I negotiate in it, which I think works well, is that I am attempting to describe the things that went through my own head in these recorded sections of time where I'm sat in front of the camera, and of course I can't do that – it's an impossible task. I am basically in a dialogue with a past self whose mental activity is more or less a mystery to me. But the fact of the tapes and their length and what happens on them – that I blink or smile or look up or down at a certain moment – is a fact that I have to negotiate now, in the present time of the performance. So I guess the other factor I have to deal with, the other person I have to negotiate with in this instance, is me, on video. It's not that different than if you are dancing to Aerosmith. Aerosmith is a thing, has a certain rhythm and tonal qualities, emotional qualities. You have to work with something like that in much the same way as I have to work with the recording of my own face. I have to deal with its absolutenesses and negotiate those.

MD: The impossibility is another way of creating tension.

TE: Yes, you set a task which you are not fully able to achieve or realise. Speaking already always involves a kind of difficulty of course; you are up against the limits of language. But I suppose, making solo performance, one might want to make sure that those kinds of conflicts, processes or difficulties are made visible, rather than erasing or hiding them. Because my fear in a solo is the sense that it all arises from the performers uncompromised or unconstrained will – this very singular 'because I want it to be like this' which is most likely quite boring. Any sense of struggle or failure or compromise or dialogue with an exterior force sounds much more promising to me than that flatness of single author-intention.

MD: Performers displaying a skill, a virtuoso comedian or a Butoh dancer, who show huge skill in one thing – I am not talking to those people in this set of interviews. Or writing about someone like Little Tich, the circus performer; a dwarf in very big boots. That was his act – circus solo work. It is a very different thing from what I am interested in here, which is how solo people are really playing with all the stuff that comes with the notion of solo ness; like virtuosity, or aloneness.

TE: I don't know, I have a level of suspicion about virtuosity and the kind of control that goes with that. And maybe in reaction to that comes this interest I am speaking about – in frailty, or in failure, or the potential for failure. This interest in process and in something that is unfolding in front of you in a slightly different kind of way – is almost a kind of political shift, isn't it? That there is something slightly distasteful politically and aesthetically about the genius stand-up comic who is just rattling through her or his material. There is something more interesting about those comedians who seem to be teetering in a certain way. That can also be virtuosic, but it negotiates that place of power differently, rather than 'I'll just crank the handle and out come all the jokes.' So what?'

MD: It's a kind of showing off, isn't it?

TE: Yeah.

MD: Which is funny. Kids get accused of that all the time.

MD: What haven't I asked you?

TE: There is something you touched on about the nature of the 'I' that is presented in those solo works; this line about there being multiple, possible I's represented, rather than a singular one. That resonates for me. I think very much in terms of versions – possible versions of oneself, possible personas. And in the pieces I often quite consciously show contradictory or different possibilities, of 'me' in this case. It's not about revealing the true version; it is much more about showing some things in between the cracks, out of which I might appear. You are not presented with a single rounded view of a person. It is much more about contradictions and layers. That seems important. And then this thing about what is true and what is not true or what is authentic and what's fictitious – also seems very important.

MD: It's a theme itself, isn't it – remembering and memory and in a way it is not about you, it is about memory. But I guess it is you in relation to it all, you in it.

TE: Yes, what I am remembering in *Words and Pictures* can be quite personal, so what I tell has an aspect of autobiographical revelation. I'm making choices about what I share and what I don't share. About how I present or construct myself.

MD: My work at the moment is *39 places I have lived*. Part of me says 'What is interesting about this? What am I doing? What is this doing?' The vehicle is the places I have lived. But there are other things going on which are important…

TE: Those list things are very explicit and transparent in one sense, but they're always more complex than they seem. When you start to list the places you've lived like that, everybody watching or listening automatically starts to make their own list. That much is always happening; that your revelation of stuff about you from the stage is greeted in part by other people going into the same imaginative cataloguing process for themselves. People are also involved in a broader consideration of how a list like that speaks to a life, how it describes or fail to describe, a life – it opens questions about identity. There is so much work there that people can do beyond the small facts and sequential narrative of where you happened to live. Perhaps as makers we are all looking for a way in which these small things can be re-tuned or focused in order to ask a question to those watching; so that they themselves can start to think and operate in a slightly different way.

MD: That is crucial and comes back to the notion of leaving space so that people can come and fill it in.

TE: Do you know Georges Perec's work? There's a collection of his called *Species of Space* which I really like. He was part of the OuLiPo group, all of them very into language games, systems and tasks. He did a lot of beautiful projects, one of which was keeping track of everything he ate for a year: so many chickens and so many peas and so many potatoes. It's self-obsessed in the most ludicrous kind of way, but somehow much more than that too.

MD: I enjoy work that rotates around people's obsessions – I find it amusing and really like that mode, obvious as it might be.

TE: Yes. Work is often criticised for being selfish or self-directed, but a lot of interesting material comes that way – in the sense that going 'in' might be a valuable route 'out' to broader questions. It's really valuable when an artist chases something that is important or interesting to them, even if it is of no immediate or obvious significance to others.

MD: It is something you have to address, the 'self' question, as a woman particularly. There is a whole history of autobiographical, confessional writing that is often assumed as all that a woman can do. 'Yes, they can write in their journals, but when it comes to real writing…' That is a history that one has to address, or at least know about.

TE: Yes, for sure. One of the exercises Perec did over many years was to go, on the last Friday of every month (or something like that), to the same cafe and describe what he saw. It's several years' worth of writing. His rubric under which that project took place was: 'Look, and if you don't see anything interesting, look again'. So the writing tasks he's setting up in this way often oblige him to identify more and more detail about the landscape and objects around him – with this stress on the uniqueness, the individual presence and identity of everything. It's an attention to detail that swims against the tide of generalisation, and pushes us to see properly, fully, what we are living in. So reading him can be fantastic. It's very personal but much more than that too – the work really makes you look at the room, and at the world, again, in a different way. I think that is what those very personal kinds of solo acts of reflection and self-reflection [do]. It is about learning to attend to the world in different ways.

MD: What is?

TE: Watching other artists, especially watching solo work, I think. It's so much about sensibility.

MD: Yes, and I am asking that question, what makes solo working particular? It isn't spoken about so much. What does it do? How does it do it?

TE: For me, as a maker, it partly goes back to what we were talking about earlier, in that working solo is a place where I can try to deal more explicitly with ideas and with thought processes that seem more or less impossible to approach or articulate in the group work I do. And secondly… (pause) I think about watching performers like Raimund Hoghe, or Meg Stuart, or Eva Meyer-Keller, or Edit Kaldor that I mentioned, so often, what I think I gain is an insight into another person's head, or a glimpse of the way that another person operates in the world. Watching solo work is a very direct encounter with a mode of being, or a sensibility. You are seeing the performer alone and you're seeing them involved in dynamic relations with tasks, objects or texts, but in some core way perhaps what you really get is to see them in an act or acts of contemplation. It's about thought processes, ways of thinking, thinking things through. Whereas group work is always about social dynamics...

The negative side [to solo working] is that you can say it is without those social forces, so it is a little bit flat – we were talking about this before. But the good thing about that flatness perhaps is that it enables the work (and the viewer) to follow much more internal logics or thought processes. Ideas and processes can be there in a rather more undramatic, uncontested way. Like your solo can be just reading out those letters or just moving a bottle and other things around on the table, because it's just you there and you are all we have to deal with. We have to accept that we go there with you. Whereas I think if you have another person in the space, these kinds of small processes are harder to buy space for – everything instantly becomes a social question. Basically being alone means that certain kinds of activity or talking are possible, where if you were trying to do those on a stage that had more people in it, you'd have to fight to get the space and that becomes a very different thing...

MD: Power and hierarchy and status is much more evident in solo work, isn't it, between audience and performer. When there are several performers on stage, you can be lower status than somebody else, can't you? There is hierarchy. You can always occupy a lower position. Whereas when you are on your own – who are you less than?

TE: I think what is also interesting about [solo work] is that the frailty and vulnerability we spoke about before can often be balanced or offset with an intimation of arrogance. As if all this evening needs is the performer, even her or his own frailty. We come back to questions around skill and virtuosity perhaps – I have [to] say that the idea of this all-mastering performer going it alone is a rather dreadful prospect. Or if someone proposes themselves in that way, you are looking forward to the moment when it will all come crashing down.

MD: Yes. Nigel does that. Nigel Charnock. I find it very interesting that he absolutely displays physical virtuosity and also includes moments where it all falls apart, when he is improvising. He consciously plays between the two.

TE: Yes, that idea of balance is the thing. In and of themselves neither extreme virtuosity nor stumbling and mumbling incompetence are that interesting for me but in the interplay is perhaps somewhere exciting.... There is something interesting there about control; about how different solo performers control or construct space and time, how they control (and let slip) audience attention. I think in solo stuff, all of the political questions about power, domination and management of the audience and so on are really very clear, because the performance is all located in one place, in one person. It is not dispersed across the whole field of the performance.

Endnotes

1. Meg Stuart is a North American choreographer and dancer based in Berlin.
2. This piece was called *Words and Pictures*.
3. Etchells' first book, *Certain Fragments*, collects some of these critical texts and performance lectures.
4. *First Night* was the first piece made by FE for mid-scale venues, in 2001, and had just been re-performed at the Toynbee Studios in 2007, prior to this interview.
5. *That Night Follows Day* was written by Etchells following workshops with Flemish children in 2007, as an invitation and commission by Flemish theatre company Victoria (now known by the name CAMPO) to make a theatre piece performed by children, for adult audiences.
6. This became *Wall of Sound* (2006), commissioned for the exhibition 'Protections' at Kunsthaus Graz in Germany. It became a two-part project in which Etchells first created a textual score from the songs sent to him and then, with choir leader Franz Jochum, formed a choir from the security guards who were working at Kunsthaus Graz and who performed live during the exhibition.
7. Ron Vawter was a North American actor, solo performer and founding member of the experimental New York-based theatre company, The Wooster Group.
8. See Lehmann, H.T. 2006. *Post Dramatic Theatre*. London: Routledge.
9. This first interview took place in 2007 – when this book is published Etchells will have been working with Forced Entertainment for thirty-three years.

Bobby Baker

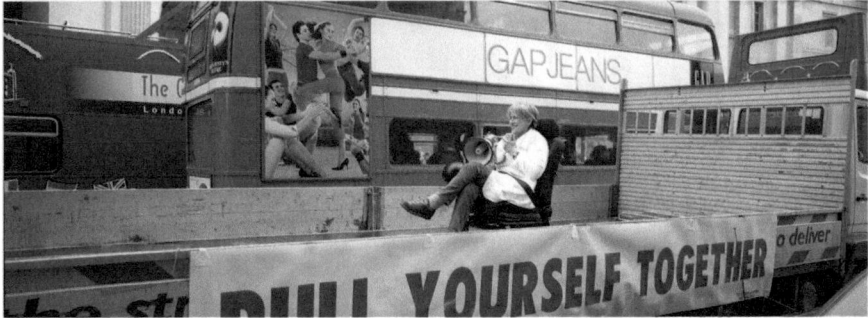

Pull Yourself Together (2000) ©Hugo Glendinning

Bobby Baker is a prolific maker of both solo and group pieces of art and performance, her artistic career spanning more than forty years. She works with sculpture, interactive installation, theatre, performance art, film, music, dance and, more recently, digital media and is renowned for her strongly visual, fiercely comic approach to performance. She trained in Fine Art at Central St Martin's School of Art, London, in the 1960s and immediately began to question the formalism prevalent in art at the time through work which was highly personal and informal. She became a performance artist early on in her career, mixing her body and her concerns as a woman and feminist into her work. Medium, means and meaning are all transposed in her work from their traditional roles. At different moments she is a chocolate-coated dancing performer, a spitting paintbrush, or a bed-sheet canvas, painted with food. Her fellow performers include people cake, or meringue ladies, as well as real breathing humans.

Her work crosses disciplines of theatre, performance art and fine art and as with all border crossers, she has received variable recognition. She wryly noted how she has been viewed by certain members of the fine arts milieu as part of 'the tumbling clowns brigade' (as a performance artist) until she later proved her fine arts credentials with her Wellcome painting exhibition in 2009. At the same time, she revealed concern about being categorised by theatre or Live Art critics as making work that 'smacks of the confessional'. Her work is much more nuanced than this implies – she uses humour and physicality to make edgy political statements as well as an autobiographical approach to reach out from the personal into wider contexts.

In this interview we focused on a period of solo working that is not written about in her book,[1] namely a series of small solo works made during an AHRC fellowship (2005–2008) at Queen Mary, London University,[2] and on her excitement at the potential exhibition of diary drawings which at the time of interview had not yet been collectively seen or published.[3] She also discussed for the first time, in depth, her long-term collaborative relationship with director and dramaturg, Palona Baloh Brown.

Interviewing Baker is similar to experiencing her work – like participating in an intimate conversation which is unpredictable, multi-levelled, and includes both laughter and fury. What leapt out at me in our conversation, coming as I do from a physical and dance theatre background, was the materiality of her practice: the right objects are found and the rest of the piece is worked out around them. Her interview is full of descriptions of making with *things*: boxes, shoes, meringues, fairy lights, flat-backed lorries, breakfast cereals, shaving foam, chocolate and sheets.[4] Baker responded frequently to questions about how she worked through narrative, through the telling of stories and offering up of images. Her background in visual art is also evident in her assertion that solo working itself is unremarkable: 'I never thought of myself as a solo artist'.

She makes use of a wide spectrum of time-scales for thinking and talking about work, as well as physical making. *Drawing on a Mother's Experience* took 'a period of three years – a very serious piece with a lot of thinking'. She revealed the expert's ability to finely judge when to engage, think, do and when to leave well alone. She is the only practitioner in these interviews who overtly discussed her use of intuition and offered several examples of how she does this – incorporating both fast 'Eureka' insights and also more considered, step-by-step intuitive working.

Baker is very clear that her work, both past and present, is solely her own vision but is then discussed, negotiated and potentially further developed through conversation with her collaborators. I was very interested to explore her long-term relationship with director and dramaturg Polona Baloh Brown, as collaboration on certain aspects of the work is a frequent, yet under-discussed practice used by solo artists. Baker's work with Brown exemplified a strong collaborative partnership between two women. It raised pertinent questions both then and now about Brown's role(s). She was variously identified as 'co-director', 'collaborator', 'director' on the Daily Life Series DV's. It would appear that her role corresponded to the current term, 'contemporary dramaturg'.[5]

An overriding impression that emerged for me from Baker's discussion of her making process was of a triangular relationship – or a 'trialogue': an interactive, dynamic, energetic exchange between herself as artist, the concept of the work and the very particular context out of which she is working: 'the process of making it had been constantly trying to check in with what is this event about, what is my personal relation to it?' (BB1: 6). The above can perhaps serve as one kind of mapping for the conversations on solo making Bobby and I had and offers contrast with how the other practitioners shaped their discussions.

Performance Chronology

From 1972 to 1980, Baker created a series of installations and performances, painting, sculpting and interacting with food as her primary creative medium. Like many other visual artists at the time, she started to include herself as a performer in her artwork, wryly locating Princess Anne's wedding day (15 November 1973) and her piece of the same name as 'a marvelously auspicious occasion on which to become a "performance artist"'.[6] A key work of that time was the installation *An Edible Family in a Mobile Home* (1976), involving life-sized cake figures eaten by audiences who walked through a caravan in her garden. In my interview, Baker references this early work as providing source material for her later piece *A Mobile Family*, in 2008. From 1980 to 1988, Baker gave birth to two children, a period of time she discusses in this interview as enabling an extended period of thinking time, culminating in her performance, *Drawing on a Mother's Experience* in 1988.

A further work *Cook Dems* followed in 1990, during which her important collaborative relationship with close friend and director, Polona Baloh Brown, started and continued on into the *Daily Life Series*. These were primarily solo works, the first being *Kitchen Show*, performed in Baker's kitchen as part of the London International Festival of Theatre (LIFT 1991). Further pieces in this series include *How to Shop* (LIFT 1993), *Take A Peek* (LIFT, South Bank Centre, London, 1995), *Grown-up School* (LIFT, Brecknock Primary School, London, 1999) and *Box Story* (LIFT, St Luke's Church, London, 2001). These performances are well documented in her book written with Michele Barrett, although she confirmed in my interview that lack of space left little room for writing about her making processes in the book. In these early performances, her signature characteristics emerge clearly. These include her complex, deliberately unstable autobiographical performance persona as 'Bobby Baker', the use of direct address, storytelling, her work with food, movement, film, multiple objects, and characteristic tones of humour, abjection, celebration and awkwardness. As with the best of autobiographical work, her performances continually evoke wider cultural concerns: questioning women's 'traditional' domains of work: motherhood, family, the home, shopping, domesticity, as well as the politics of health and mental illness. The subsequent large-scale group piece *How to Live* (Barbican Theatre, London, 2004) marked the beginning of her increased focus on mental health issues. From 2005 to 2008 she took part in the three-year AHRC fellowship at Queen Mary, University College of London, making several small-scale solos: *Ballistic Buns*, *Mad Meringues* and *The Meringue Ladies Sing ABBA's I Believe in Angels*. This fellowship culminated in her making a collaborative pilot piece with actor and choreographer Sian Stevenson, *A Model Family* (2008), and several other group pieces, including *Give Peas A Chance* and *First FEAT*. Continuing to explore issues of mental health, Baker went on to tour *Mad Gyms and Kitchens* in the UK in 2012 and 2013 and more recently obtained crowd funding to make a series of animations – *The Roxi and Rudi Roadshow*, which publicises the continuous arts and mental health programme produced by her company, Daily Life Limited.

Artist website: http://www.bobbybakersdailylife.com

The Interview

MD: Are you working on a solo at the moment?

BB: You use the word 'solo' in a very precise way. I had not been aware of using that word myself. I work with other people in so many different ways these days and really revel in that. One of the ideas about applying for a Fellowship at Queen Mary[7] was that I had a few ideas I wanted to experiment with, that were less grand in scale. I had got into this increasingly epic cycle of doing shows that, because of the very concept of them, as with *How to Live*, was about being on the Barbican main stage to launch my own Therapy Empire, and about being grandiose. I wanted to do things that were more off the cuff, going back to how I worked in the 70s. So when I went to Queen Mary, I got that chance. Pol[8] and I had amicably moved onto doing other sorts of work. But there I was at Queen Mary and there was no budget, like it was in the 70s. Since the mid 90s all the shows needed funding. It was interesting to try simple ideas for a while.

MD: What date was that?

BB: My fellowship started in 2005. I was one of the 'artists in residence' at Queen Mary, in 2006. I did a piece called *Ballistic Buns*. But people worked with me on that – like they made a short film and sound track. Does that count?

MD: It absolutely does. All the people I am talking to have collaborated.

BB: I used to do everything myself in the 70s. Like *Edible Family [in a Mobile Home* 1976]. I come from a fine art background and those traditions underpin my work. At that stage, in order for anything to be authentic, I had to make literally everything. Luckily I let that go. So one of [the] early events during my fellowship was at the PSI 12[9] at Queen Mary, 'Performing Rights', about human rights, in June 2006. I did various things and one of them was *Ballistic Buns*, during the opening plenary session. They had various shows: Lois Weaver, the Red Ladies and all sorts. I performed *Ballistic Buns*, which was about my grandparents and World War One – anorexia and breakdowns. It was a really simple piece. It's a kind of small element leading up to *Model Family* (pilot 2008). I did all this thinking about the history of women, on one side of my family, through my mother, and they were all pretty fucked up and angry. Then there was my grandfather, who was a ballistic engineer. My mother was dying then, slowly. She died in the autumn – she was 92. I wanted to find out information about the family. I was prodding and she started to hand on bits of information. I started to go up to Newcastle where she comes from and asked questions and met a few people who are still alive from her generation. I had a fascination with the bits of information I had, and from knowing my grandmother. I used to go to her after school for tea when my mum was working and she was a very complex and fucked up woman who was anorexic all her life. I think I had the idea before the conference on human rights. I had made the application to the AHRC and got the funding and said I wanted to do these small experimental shows.

I know where I had the idea! It was the year before. I was physically and mentally very ill. My mother had had a heart attack and I had done an absurd amount of touring during one nine-month period – I had five admissions to psych places. It was a bloody nightmare – two were in this wonderful women's crisis house called Drayton Park, but three in hospital. That was the first time that I had ever been in a psychiatric hospital and God forbid it ever happens again. I mean I was physically burnt out. We had been to China, Australia and America in that period. I did by then know that I had got the fellowship and financial security for the next three years, but it was too late. I was exhausted in every sense. It was a ghastly hospital – terrible abuse of human rights. With the staff bullying me, it echoed parts of my childhood, so it was a like entering a replication of how things had been in my family for generations. I was stuck in this room, luckily on my own, and I was thinking about the future and I knew PSI was going to be the following summer. So what I retreated to (a lot of these ideas come when I am under pressure from something external) I retreated to thinking about the future and critical pieces of work I was going to make.

MD: How interesting – the word 'retreat'.

BB: Actually I had forgotten that, because there is a drawing of me lying on the bed, and all these little glimpses of ideas, and one of them is of

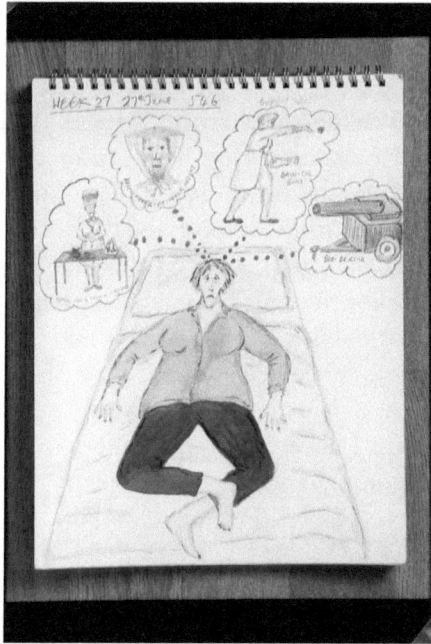

Day 546, Bobby Baker's Diary Drawings: Mental Illness and Me, 1997–2008
©Bobby Baker

me chucking buns… I literally cracked up laughing. I was physically ill but also stuck in this room, people looking through the window, having the worst time of my whole life for seven weeks. Trying to get out, and so retreating into thinking about ideas was just *joyful.* Laughing at the ideas. So I entirely made that show in that hospital bedroom. That is extraordinary, that I had forgotten that. Even the title. I remember texting it to somebody – calling it *Ballistic Buns* because my grandfather was a ballistic engineer.

MD: When you say you entirely made it in a room. Was that in your head?

BB: Yeah. When you come back again I will show you a diary drawing I did then. I can't remember what the other thought bubbles were – five of them – they all have turned out to be things that I went on to make. It was happiness to do it, because it was about a complex set of ideas. *Ballistic Buns* is about my grandmother's anorexia and my grand-father's breakdown, and her odd relationship with food and how she used to chuck buns. She wanted to be an artist essentially, but was denied that opportunity and taken on a cruise instead. What I talked about was a very potted bit of history that has informed my thinking about family history, and ideas for future work. The piece had to be some-thing like seven or eight minutes long and I chose a piece of music – the Ukulele Orchestra of Britain playing the Dambusters theme, while I throw buns at the audience shouting 'Catch!' What was so extraordinary was that it actually worked. I did it a year later and then again a year later at Arts Admin. That sequence of ideas that I lay on that bed and dreamt up, worked so well. Why it came together was that there were elements related to lots of things I have done before. So it was not entirely a new leap into something completely new.

MD: How did it relate to what you had done before?

BB: Food. Telling stories based on my experience and a particular way of engaging with the audience. Knowing how I would phrase and discuss it. I could imagine exactly how I would be – the finale with a piece of music and me doing something extreme. Formally, it was a structure that I had done versions of before. I think in these small pieces I have picked up techniques that I have used before ... Another piece I did as 'artist in residence' at PSI was *Mad Meringues*. It was at the finale of the whole conference. Oh, it was fun! I used a university buggy with a driver from Queen Mary, which is the only campus university in London. Charlie Whittuck, my son, made a platform to go on the back and I made several hundred meringue women holding international flags – 'Mad Women of the World' – who had come to wave everyone off. There was an absurdly big ghetto blaster strapped to the top of the buggy, blasting out a Welsh Voice Choir singing 'Sweet Chariots of Fire'. We just zapped around, serving the meringues. What was interesting about that was I wasn't dis-cussing any of it with Pol. It was a scary, weird feeling of being entirely on my own again – liberating and anarchic – but odd. It was on the edge of chaos but wasn't quite and wonderful at times. I went on and did three or four more small pieces at Queen Mary ... I think it is having the context of doing things there, where things can just happen ...

There is a third piece I think may also be interesting to talk about. A really unusual short piece I did at about the same time was at the Theatre Museum, London. Elaine Aston and Gerry Harris from Lancaster had arranged a London conference or seminar as part of their three-year project.[10] They invited five of us, women artists, to be on a panel. Age wise – I was the oldest and then four younger women. Elaine and Gerry asked if I could I do some sort of performance thing to mark the occasion. Their audience were mostly younger women – about eighty people. It was a really charged, interesting atmosphere. Again I was in this stage of massively overworking due to commitments and money. I knew Elaine had had this season of having people running workshops about how they work. They had done a book to accompany the programme of work. I hadn't seen the book. I really didn't know what the hell to do and I wasn't sure what I felt about it and I was fed up … all this discussion about work and about women. I had been doing this so long, and overworking, it was very relevant and yet [I thought], 'Oh God do we still have to keep doing this, why haven't things changed?' I looked at their website and I wasn't sure what I felt about it because there were these images of angels. I thought 'Oh God angels, what do I think about angels?' I suppose I was quite angry about the amount of work I had, trying to increase my funding and the position I was in in relation to other companies. It was a sort of battling phase, a period of reflecting about my age and generation and gender. I had not bothered much to battle in ways that other people had, who were either male or younger. I was somehow very annoyed with myself. So that was the context. I wanted to resurrect the *Meringue Ladies*. I came up with this idea. I thought – I haven't got very much time. I could probably make a hundred of them and it was quite clear from the conversations on the phone with the technical guy it was going to be an unpredictable situation practically. I didn't know which space it would be in and I didn't know what would be available. I said I needed a table and a power socket but I could tell it was going to be risky. We couldn't get in until an hour before. So there I was, a couple of nights before and thinking about this group of women, these meringues who represented women artists and practitioners and the idea of them being angels. Of course they are little, blobby, plump, sugar figures. I listened to music that I have hanging around which makes me laugh. There is an ABBA track called 'I could be an angel' or something like that …

MD: 'I Believe in Angels'?

BB: 'I Believe in Angels', that's right. I am hopeless at the words but it was that saccharine sort of wonderful music that appeals to my cynical side …

MD: 'Something good in every one I see'.

BB: Yes exactly. If you listen to the words you could see how it mirrored this anger and fury. So I did a really risky, odd thing. I came up with this idea and I thought – this is what I am going to ask people to do. There was a lot of sharpness. I sort of imagined, which proved to be right, that it would be a very enthusiastic group of people. I assumed they would be mostly younger women. I was worried that it might be a harsh piece but it was bringing together my confusion or anger but also how moving the whole situation was. It was very much mirroring where Gerry and Elaine had got to; where women were as artists and why so many of them worked alone, although I hadn't read the book by then. So what I actually did was… My son was around and he is a sculptor, so I said, 'Have you got any lighting I could use?'

MD: Had you made the 100 meringues by then?

BB: Yes, in three batches – it takes about a day. You make them and leave them, spaced over two or three days. I tend to make them at night. So I asked him if he had any lighting around. He looked in a cupboard and in a biscuit tin there was this battery-operated fairy light thing in a circle. It was perfect. So I used that. I had the meringues. I had this piece of music and a ghetto blaster.

I headed off in a cab and we got stopped because there was some enormous London public event. Everyone got stuck on the tube. Elaine and Gerry had got stuck too. So God, it was like – 'I don't work like this anymore, I am in my fifties. I should be more organised than this'. Yet that was also very exhilarating. I didn't know what was going to happen. We found a lovely little marble table with iron legs. We set up the meringues, the light, plugged it in, worked out how to turn it on and off, fiddled with the ghetto blaster and that was it. I hadn't practised it. Then we went off and did the panel discussion. There was an air of reverence and also a great joy that we were all together and talking about these things. In the back of my mind I had this idea of what I was going to ask people to do. So then Elaine and Gerry said 'Bobby, I gather you have an event for us. It's wonderful. Bobby has set up something'. I had put a cloth over the meringues and I said 'ok', and I asked everyone to stand around them. I was rather bossy so they all had to stand around in a circle and look at this little table and I took the cloth off and switched the lights on and there was a gasp because they are beautiful – the meringues, when there are a group of them. I had worked out how to make all sorts of women of colour – I am quite excited by the techniques. They were a group of women of the world really. So there was everybody's expectation and delight and I introduced the idea of angels. I said, 'just look at the meringues and I want you to listen to the music – its four and a bit minutes and this is a durational piece. I want us all to smile the whole way through. Just look at the meringues. If you can't bear it, you can go away, if you can't keep the smile. But if you stay here, you have to smile.' They looked really shocked, and bewildered. It was an extraordinary experience. Elaine phoned me from the train, and said, 'What was *that* about Bobby? I don't know, but I found it incredibly moving and sad'. I said – 'yeah'.

I felt rather cruel in a way but it was just so exhilarating because it was very related to the process of making. I had been constantly trying to check in with what this event was about, what my personal relation to it was. I was one of the oldest people there and excited about my work but the reality was I was having very big problems with money and status. The status to get the money or even the self-confidence to get better core funding because I was brought up to be 'pathetically grateful' to have anything at all. Yet I still can't do what I want to do. Also observing the situation in the world, comparing myself to male artists my age, and much more widely and importantly, the situation of women in the world. What goes on, as in rape etc. So it was a harsh piece. It was coming up with something which, just for that moment in time, worked in a particular way. I don't know what people took away with them, but it was very exhilarating for me. I'd never want to do it again.

MD: It's a one off?

BB: That is what I am interested in. Doing things, and then that's it. Alongside projects which are much bigger in scale.

MD: In terms of making that piece of work, you have described the context and sources and things that were important to you and how to weave those into an event. When did you decide to ask people to smile?

BB: It was when I listened to the music. It made me laugh, because it was so cheesy. I mean I love cheesy music. Also the words were so ironic and sad. A few people had tears in their eyes. I nearly cried. It's always trying to get that edge. So then, the idea of getting people to smile, if they stayed in the group. To stand in the group was the last decision. It was the edge. It gave it the edge.

MD: Can you remember when you decided that?

BB: No. A lot of those sorts of ideas happen when I am on my own in the kitchen. Actually, it is usually in the kitchen. I would set myself a problem. Sometimes ideas arrive completely formed, but generally there is something I want to communicate or there is an idea for a context and then it's a question of thinking, 'well, what is this about? Oh – that's the question then'.

MD: An idea for a context?

BB: My work is mostly based on ideas that I have generated myself or thought of a setting to chase after. But I suppose the ones I am describing at this stage are related to the Fellowship. So those pieces respond to an invitation.

MD: I like 'responsive'.

BB: Yeah, so you can sense a context and a framework and how you can relate to that. So you have a starting point. It's a question of having one idea and then thinking 'what's next?' Having a question. So the question might be 'do we have any music' and then thinking about it and then toying around with that idea and listening to some music and then thinking, 'yes that takes it a bit further'. It's a step-by-step process. But the most enjoyable bit is thinking 'I don't know so I am not going to think about it now, I am just going to put it away in my head', and then 'Ping', hopefully it just pops out or you look at it and you think 'no I don't know' and you put it away again, and you go on until you find a solution.

MD: What is the 'ping' that happens?

BB: It just happens. The weirdest thing is when I often can't remember how I got to it. I just don't understand where some ideas come from. It is just having a set of ideas or a feeling about something and it arrives: out of my unconscious or the setting, or a train of thought. I don't really bother about it actually. But it is lovely. It's always very surprising, quite often things I don't want to do. Like putting the anchovies into my mouth.[11] I think 'Oh I don't want to do that'. But actually when I look back on it, it was the solution. But when it comes to, say, pieces like *Drawing on a Mother's Experience* (1988)[12] which I thought about over a period of three years, that involves a lot of serious thinking. Step by step by step.

MD: Compared to the making of some of your earlier works, do you feel that there is something really different about what you are doing in these smaller works?

Drawing on a Mother's Experience (first performed 1988) ©Andrew Whittuck and Bobby Baker

BB: What was interesting was that *Drawing on a Mother's Experience* was a piece that came out of eight years of not making work, and was based on experiences that I had earlier. But when it comes to the way I am working now, I feel incredibly privileged because I have had all this experience of working with Pol, of endlessly discussing ideas or the way I am or the way I present myself and constantly having the feedback from somebody I trust, as an outside eye. What we enjoyed with *Box Story* (2001) or any of those early shows that toured and toured was to go to a place where we weren't familiar with the setting. It could be abroad or anywhere – not knowing what was going to happen and then having the opportunity to repeat and learn and adjust and adapt the show. So I have gained this huge backlog of experience. I worked on my own and got a bit of confidence and then almost losing that confidence in the process of making bigger work and relying on Pol, and then gradually moving towards a point of being much more crisp and clear about decisions. Trusting intuition essentially. That is what it came back to.

Now I'm experimenting with coming back to a state of thinking 'I just want to do these really impromptu things', with this irreverence that I never had, but also a confidence and actually like 'fuck em, I don't mind if it doesn't work, I don't mind. I just want to take risks again'. Because what had been so glorious in the 70s, it was just constantly taking risks and not caring what people thought. I, like other people, had removed myself from the arena where one was judged and reviewed because I didn't want to be part of that. So, to go back to being in that position just feels wonderful. It's like sketching. Having the freedom to do that. That is what I like about working on my own, from time to time...

MD: What is the role of your self in your solo work?

BB: It was always my terror, with *Drawing on a Mother's Experience*, when it took off, that somebody would say that – the 'smack of the confessional'. I was going to Edinburgh and I read a review of someone else's solo piece; that it 'smacked of the confessional box'. I was horrified. Pol would often ask: 'is this self-indulgent?' I actually think that it is a very important tension to keep. 'Why am I doing this, is it self-indulgent?' Sometimes one does stray into that, definitely, and you always have to come back to – 'What is this about?' It always comes back to – 'well I only know this from my point of view, I don't know if anyone will relate to it'. That is the risk. So that's just the way I am. I can't go much further than that because I don't work in another way.

MD: Fiction, fact; real, not real. What is your self and what is not your self? It is a deliberately crude question and people answer it in different ways.

BB: It is sort of accepting I am middle aged and middle class and white. I live in Islington, I grew up in the suburbs. That is who I am.

MD: You are aiming to do something that people can relate to, with their own stories. I read that in your book – that you want people to go out on the street after a performance and talk about their own stories. I am interested in what makes you into that sort of maker?

BB: I am thinking of Sarah Kane for instance. The form she used was writing, of which she was sublimely good. But you wouldn't have people say that ['smacks of the confessional'] – because it is high art, it is writing. Yet it is based on her own internal world and her mental state. I relate to it very strongly, having been in places that she was in mentally. Autobiographical work is seen as lacking a status and yet it is where new ideas and new forms come from. So one has to put up with people being snooty about it because that has always been the way of the world. It used to get up my nose a lot but it doesn't now because I think – we will show you, we will show you.

MD: What interests me is you saying, 'that is what you do…'. Why does one do that instead of write a play? Or direct?

BB: It strikes me that there are a lot of young women who want to work in this way. Quite often they will work in twos or threes. I think it is essentially about stepping outside the way work is traditionally made and finding a way of communicating ideas that don't quite fit other forms. When you talk about wanting to express something that makes you very angry. How would you do that otherwise? You could make a documentary, you could write a novel, you could write a play but there is something about your feelings yourself, that requires you to physically do it yourself. Do you see what I mean?

BB: It [autobiographical performance] is obviously a matter of interest because people do it and you obviously do it. It's comic. Who are you? I get into a group of people and the way I communicate it is like giving a speech. It's all me. I just am. I can adapt it and play with it. It is all me…

And there is also a sort of strangeness about certain ideas. Like putting a tin of anchovies in my mouth. I wouldn't do it now.

MD: The sense I got from you speaking about this before is that you had to do it.

BB: All those different voices you have in your head, from your upbringing. Part of me is really wanting to be normal, to not stick out and really disapproving of things. Not judgemental, but quite shook up by things that are odd. They are sort of alarming and I wonder 'why should I do that?' Come on, grow up'. I am really not going to do that because it is stupid or silly. There is certainly that bit of me. The most puzzling thing of all is just being absolutely convinced that people can connect with it. That is almost the most scary bit and that is why I have to do it, because I know it will work. But I don't know why it will work. I know it is about a very complex set of things and if I sat down and thought and read, I would probably understand it. But it is the oddness of thinking 'this is freaky and weird and a bit strange. It's perfect for this show because it communicates'.

MD: Would it change it if you tried to put it into words?

BB: Oh yeah. If I was a writer. I would go down that route. But I'm not, that's not my talent. The whole point is that it is a way of communicating ideas in another way. The polar opposite of being concerned and worried and 'suburban' about what I am doing is to then get very annoyed when someone calls me eccentric. I can get defensive.

MD: The problem with that is that the person is putting themselves forward as being an expert on what is 'normal'.

BB: But that is how people think. I completely agree with you – every time that happens I get annoyed.

MD: A really good friend of mine calls me odd or eccentric sometimes. I think it is actually an arrogant thing to say. It assumes where she is, is normal. I am not trying to do anything 'normal' or not normal... I am simply expressing something that needs saying.

BB: So I go into a reverie about that but I don't want to be like that, essentially. I mean I want to be an artist and I like to be the sort of person

I am, but I don't want to be seen as odd or different or eccentric. I find it really offensive. Not offensive. Judgemental. Exactly like you say. But it's odd because I am actually doing both things at the same time.

MD: Yes. And for me, I draw on that split.

BB: Do you?

MD: Well. In a way. There is something very self-conscious about labelling something as eccentric or odd and narrowing. It reminds me of people calling me 'exotic'. Exotic to what? Eccentric to what? So what is 'normal – standard'? Caucasian, or Black. 'Pure bred'?

BB: The bit in your questions I liked was, 'What is your favourite solo piece?' Your mind goes 'woooooo'. It has to be Tommy Cooper... Egg, bag, bag egg, egg bag, Bag egg. I can't remember – it's just like egg bag bag egg – so much laughter. Patricia Riley (who performed in *How To Shop*) was on the boards since she was 13 and she knew Tommy. They would turn up at variety places over the years and she was a soprano at that stage and tells some hysterical stories. It was very straightforward – it was his living and he had to earn money. That was what he did. He was clearly like that on and off stage. In and out of all sorts of moods – that is what he did for a living and enjoyed it.

MD: What is it about that particular piece, then?

BB: It's so abstract. I mean what did it mean? It didn't mean anything. It is about a commentary on magic. Magicians. It's just nonsensical.

MD: The Newspaper Rip Gag. That was the one that made me chuckle.

BB: What did he do?

MD: He just tears a piece of newspaper into bits. It's meant to be like origami or newspaper dolls or something 'creative' and he starts with careful ripping and then just switches to tearing it all up. I also love him laughing at himself. I noticed that is something that you do in your work.

BB: I very occasionally do talks about the work. I do find 'Spitting Mad' funny and there are people behind me and I can't stop laughing. It's awful – laughing at your own jokes. But I think laughing is a great way to be, isn't it? Marina writes about it brilliantly.[13] When I look back at women in my family, they all did that. Laughed. I never knew why I did that. But now I understand it as being about power. It's rebellious and irreverent and also very liberating.

MD: Can we talk about collaboration within your solo practice? Your long relationship with Polona Baloh Brown, in particular?

BB: Initially, after the eight-year gap in making my own work, I was looking for people to help with the administration side of things but not for making the work. The reason Pol came on board was that I couldn't manage alone. I was finding it so difficult with this mini tour in Glasgow – *Cook Dems*, all of which I won't repeat because it is in my book.[14] Pol and I had been friends for a long time. We are very fond of each other, quite alike: bossy, control freaks. We had had (which I think can be the sign of a good relationship) two or three really big rows. We agreed it was because we were close. People who knew us were quite worried when Pol suggested coming up and keeping me company. But it was wonderful. What was really interesting was that I wouldn't let her do anything practical – I don't know how she put up with it. For *Drawing on a Mother's Experience* and *Cook Dems*, we toured endlessly and spent an enormous amount of time together. If she got the props ready for *Cook Dems*, I would redo everything. I would repack the bag. It was terrible. It was almost a ritual, a habit stemming from working on my own. Her role in terms of making the work is so complex, because it changed and evolved over time.

There was this period of her being very 'hands off'. To sum it up: I needed support, an outside eye, which was what ultimately she said she was, and acted brilliantly at it. But it was more than that, because she contributed and worked very closely on creating *How to Shop* and *Take a Peek, Grown Up School* and *Box Story – Take a Peek* most of all.[15] For the DVD series,[16] her credits change. It seemed to make sense to use historical credits to describe her role. We had agonised debates with each show about what to credit her with in marketing material. There wasn't the right word. There was not an easy way to describe what she was doing. The way we worked together seemed new, and very female.

MD: People use the phrase 'outside eye'.

BB: She comes from a theatre background, so she was more specific about what words meant. Coming from a fine art background, there was no such role as hers. She would be equating it to a director but also saying 'I am not a director, I am not a writer – I am not a dramaturg'. Festivals were really unhelpful about crediting her. They were not interested in what we were explaining, and we had endless battles. When we were preparing the DVDs, it seemed best to leave it as it was in the programme.

What was interesting was that it reflected how we were working at that time. *Kitchen Show* was the first thing we seriously worked on together. That was slightly hands off and then [her role] developed, because we toured it so much. Then we gradually worked more closely on the content of shows. Say for example, *Take a Peek*. I can't remember what the exact titling was, but she was so closely involved – collaborating. It was something we shared, about being a woman and in *How to Shop* she was also very involved. Over those years I learnt a lot from her and I also slightly lost myself at times. I could never work with anyone else in that role now. We would have endless discussions, she would ask me 'what is your gut feeling?' It essentially always stemmed from my vision but with an unquantifiable contribution from her. I would say she worked on both the making of the work and how I came across as a person, my persona.

So it was the performance element and the making of the work. Those were the two [main] strands. The third thing that came in very strongly with the work on mental illness was her acting like a dramaturg. She would act in a third way, by being the audience. I would do all this talking – endlessly – and she would say 'I have lost interest, you are boring me – I don't understand that word.' It was a kind of an endless process of pruning and adapting.

MD: It would be interesting to hear even more specifically what you two did.

BB: Well for instance, in *Kitchen Show*, it was very early days of us working together. We were down in Dorset, because we used to go and stay there with the kids. She said, 'you could do this as an ending' and I said 'no, that is not how I see it'. It was very tentative to begin with, how she could engage or not. I suppose as our trust grew, it generally worked with us having discussions. We talked endlessly about preparation: how to make the show, because it was launching in LIFT which was high profile. We didn't work so closely together – it was not as intense as it became with *How to Shop* and *Take a Peek* and to an extent *Grown Up School*. That was the next phase. *Kitchen Show* was very much a personal show – it was what I thought about daily life at that stage. We evolved the performance and it became more stylised as time went on. I certainly felt at the time that the joy was having a show that was made and then touring it and working together and her sitting there night after night. I trusted her entirely and she would come back and say, 'oh yes or… '. It was a very close relationship.

MD: So she would watch you and then come and talk to you.

BB: Yes and we developed a pattern – we would talk and walk through the show in the space where it was going to be. We would talk about the last time I had done it and ways I could adapt it to whatever environment I was in. That is what interested us most, in another country, [for example], what was relevant and how would we adapt it to the environment? It was always ad-libbed, to a degree. There was always an element of it being new every time. That was the really enjoyable bit, apart from spending lots of time together. She is very good company, and we liked to be away and we liked to talk about life. I can only say positive things. It became more complicated later on when we had to involve other people.

How to Shop was very complicated, for example. It was a very ambitious show. Carole Lamond came in – as a filmmaker. It was pretty positive. I would work with Carole and the three of us got on well together. Carole suggested doing the drawings like a storyboard. I had a lot of things in my head and I did these drawings that were in the book.[17] That was incredibly helpful. Steve Wald, who is my technical director, started working with us again. Then we had the two actors. We were both unsure and very tentative about that. I remember splashing foam and being pregnant. I had got this obsession with the image of smelling my father's shaving soap. It was quite phallic. Pol and I got this idea of using spray foam. I remember being in her garden and we suddenly got this idea and I can't say whose idea it was, of me being pregnant and slapping foam.

I don't know if she could say who got that idea. It was utterly us working together. So we tried it out in the garden and we both had to come and rest. We were so astonished with what we had made. It was a joy that used to happen: trying it and it worked.

MD: Was this done through talking? Was that your method?

BB: Oh totally. We would never try anything out until we had talked about it. I would have all of the ideas – I would tell her the ideas. I used to be so on edge about how she would respond, I would have to go and have a rest on her sofa. She would get some lunch. I would sleep for half an hour because I was so exhausted with the intensity and the nervousness of how she would respond.

MD: So that was *How to Shop*.

BB: *Take a Peek* was a development, and I think it was much more successful. *How to Shop* worked but it had points that were not quite resolved.

MD: Once you had devised it, did you then perform and she would be an outside eye again – did she take that role?

BB: Yes, all the way through, everywhere we toured. Right up to *Box Story* and into *How to Live* but then she handed over half-way through.

MD: Is it possible for you to give me a concrete example of a day? What she would do – what you would do?

BB: With *Take a Peek*, we had worked out all of these stages, from endless discussions – like the one about eating plums. I would say – 'well I have got this idea – it's kind of about abortion and the foetus, after the rape scene, when we throw nuts at my mouth. I was thinking I am going to spit them'. So we got bottled plums. I have a plum tree and I would bottle them occasionally, in a rather frenzied way. So I got one and she said 'well, go and try it, go and try it'. We were in one of our kitchens, because we always worked in our kitchens. I put it in my mouth and I spat it out at her. She was screaming with laughter and we both agreed – yes it's disgusting and really revolting and its vile and female. So that is the way we would work.

Box Story (2001) ©Andrew Whittuck and Bobby Baker

Box Story was wonderful. It was the best of the lot because by then we had done the others. I had this idea for years – a clear image of carrying that huge box in.[18] Absolutely exactly. I got the idea from having a fridge freezer delivered and it was in a huge box – they are usually made for the show but that is the packaging for fridge freezers and I remember being out in the road and getting very excited about the box. It was years before I did the show but it connected a whole range of ideas to do with a sarcophagus and stuff. So I had that idea and I had the idea of wearing it – climbing in it and the packages and boxes. So there was a really long period before the show. Pol was working on another show for a couple of years and I remember getting very concerned that I hadn't worked out what would happen in the middle. I had no idea it would be putting things on the floor. I assumed I wanted to make something out of boxes. The process I have for thinking about these things these days, which I presume is a more conscious development of what went on before but with much less anxiety involved, is to think of a problem and not get anxious, but to try and establish what the question is. 'Question' is a bit general. But to think 'what is it I am I looking for?' and then just shutting my mind down and putting it away. Then it pops up, when you have got time to think, like when driving. But absolutely not to focus on it but get on with life.

I did start to get quite panicky. How am I going to resolve this? I had got all these ideas about making a sculpture out of the boxes, out of food and every time I tested something, it wouldn't work. So there I was in the 'pop up' stage. I was going around Waitrose, shopping. I love packaging. I was looking at cereal bars. It is quite posh in Waitrose, and there was this wonderful box. It had all the ingredients, photographed in rows. They were all clumped: cornflakes, grains, nuts and raisins. It was a stunning image, just on the edge of the pack. It made you want to buy it but I also found it was beautiful, and I looked at it and I just went oooh. It was an extraordinary moment. I remember getting really, really excited. I didn't really know what it was but I just knew it was part of the answer. I was cycling a lot. I cycled to the day centre. I remember being sort of rather day-dreamy. I was so absorbed with this idea and every so often it would pop up: 'what am I going to do? Why is this a good idea? What am I going to do with these little arrangements, ingredients, the contents of the boxes?' All that coming from a photograph on the side of a package. I was putting on my ankle clips and it just suddenly went 'boom' – this airborne map of the world. It was an extraordinary moment. It was so extraordinary I will never forget it because I knew exactly where I was standing.

MD: Did you see it as an image?

BB: No, it was a concept of a map. It was not an image of what it was at all. I didn't know how it would be until we started rehearsing with it.

MD: So what did you see?

BB: I saw a set of ideas – actions, really. It was the connections suddenly between what I was doing with the story of my life, all the strands that were there for a long time and I suddenly made this connection – mapping. It was about making sense of something by mapping it. So it was essentially looking down on it. But I wouldn't have said that I had actually thought much about mapping before. It was such an unusual thing to think. I don't know what had happened in order for that to pop into my mind. But it seemed to instantly connect: 'We can make a map of the world, connected with the whole Pandora myth, connected with everything to do with the of Christianity and how it is now. The image in the stain glass window in the church [where we were working under-pinned some ideas too.] Jesus is standing on a miniature world – his bare feet on green grass and a little island that is clearly meant to be the world, with the sea around it'. So – the map and the world, connected with the whole imagery of godliness, without going through all the references. The universe. That was a very exciting moment.

Then I cycled home thinking about it and I got to this next stage of worrying: 'Oh, no I will have to draw, I will have to draw a map.' I had done that before, with *Drawing on a Mother's Experience*. I thought, 'Oh no I can't repeat myself'. I was concerned but not for long, as I suddenly remembered that one of the whole points of doing the show was to revisit that idea and go through its central story. Then I thought, 'Oh it's alright then', and I knew it was very different. It was not a map in abstract like Jackson Pollock – it was a map. It wasn't going to be on a cloth. It was definitely going to be on the ground. That was the shock of it, throwing food onto the floor... I had made all these decisions about the shoes and the overall. I had these stories. I had resolved this knotty problem about the boxes – what to do with content of boxes. I knew I had to make an artwork. I decided it had to be sculptural. Pol came in later on and we dis-cussed it. We worked on it in the church. It was very joyful. We were united in what we were doing. I had various stories on the go, because I couldn't set the structure... The way it worked was that we had a long discussion about the pros and cons and how people would react and how to play it and she would go off and we would meet a week later and by then I had thought, 'no it has got to be chronological and we will see what happens'. I remember the bit with the box because by then, we were in the church. We had a few months before the actual show. We had one box made. I had a knife. I didn't know what to do... Then I don't know how that decision got made but I got in and cut holes and as I was cutting holes, I thought of the shapes and then we both fell about laughing again, you know, because it worked. She probably remembers it because she was watching it. She said 'well actually you are going to have to get your legs out – how are you going to do that?' So it was very much a conversational thing.

Then all that was set and we did the actual making of the show, in a church. I had a terrific amount of anxiety, about how you start the show. It was very important to get the tone right. What was odd was that I got it completely wrong. I worked out the imagery but every time I came out of the vestry, I imagined Graham Norton. It was the shoes – blue stiletto shoes with jewels on. I remember Pol said 'why are you talking in that weird way? Why don't you just be yourself?' I said – 'Oh yes, are you sure?' Even in the early days of performing it, I would go back to a bit of Graham at the beginning. Pol was right. It was completely wrong to do it in a camp way. I kept on saying, 'But Pol I have this feeling, are you sure?' and we did it again and again and I knew it wasn't quite right. In the end I decided I had done it as a way of dealing with the Edna-type glamour,[19] to make it into a camp thing...

MD: Why did you have to wear those particular shoes?

BB: Those shoes were just essential. I had searched everywhere and found them in New Bond Street. It was a very expensive shoe shop full of glamorous people. Like in *How to Shop* I knew it had to be those white slingbacks. I think it has become a little bit laboured, in a way, the shoe thing, but it's a kind of a statement. It does actually change who you are if you have got a different pair of shoes on.

MD: So you were describing to me the Graham Norton thing and having to be 'in drag' to wear those shoes.

BB: It was obviously an intuitive way of dealing with being so sexually feminised in clippy-cloppy stiletto heels. I think I became more comfortable wearing the shoes the more I performed that show.

MD: The Graham Norton character disappeared?

BB: Well, it was drummed out of me because it was so wrong. I think we had two rehearsal blocks, so we did it and then we had a gap and then we came back. I was very tense about whether it would work. I think that heightened the over-acting in a way. I do remember a comment from Steve.[20] We have worked together a long time and he is very succinct in what he says. We were touring, the three of us, and he said, 'Good, it is you at last' and I thought 'Ooh I wish he had said it before' but at the same time I couldn't have just started doing the show just being me. We toured that one a lot, and it was the best of the best. We enjoyed it, Pol, me and Steve – touring like that and talking about politics and ideas.

MD: How many weeks did it take you to make that?

BB: I had been thinking about it for years. I was probably working with Pol for nine months. We tended to meet once a week. Then we had three weeks solidly working on it before it opened. We had a fabulous time with Joc.[21] That was the first time we worked with her. I had established a relationship with her while Pol was away. It just worked. We spaced it out. The way I prefer to work is to have a bit of time [together] and then have a couple of months thinking and then come back to it. Stage it out over a period of time so there is lots of thinking time. We had a period of time in the church with Joc where we grew to understand each other. She watched a run through. She then went off and wrote the specific music. It was incredible. The whole thing about that show was comfortable. We just got on very well, the three of us. Then she involved other musicians.

MD: What I would now like to ask you more about is 'thinking as making' and making strategy. It may not be as conscious as 'strategy' but you speak a lot about thinking as making. Like you said in *Drawing on a Mother's Experience* that you thought about it for three years. And *Box Story*, for ten years. You also talked about making like this when you were in hospital. A colleague of mine told me about a performer, Australian-born Margaret Cameron, who had talked to him about making a piece of work by sitting on a sofa, thinking a whole performance out and then doing it. Other people do it completely differently – they try it out repeatedly, or they start with improvised movement and see what happens.

BB: In making live work, mostly it's thinking. I couldn't even say it's to do with painting because there are people who paint and paint and paint. Many of my favourite painters over-paint. They don't have that kind of certainty; they do a lot of sketches and plans.

MD: At Dartington, we don't encourage students to think too much, because they can fall into a 'sit around and chat about it' mode.

BB: You can get completely paralysed into not doing anything. I met a young woman when we were doing Bonkersfest. I said 'just do it, just do something'. She had left college and there is that awful bit when you leave – just horrible. I said – 'Show anything – just do something'. It's a balance. It's also very financial. Andrew[22] and I have spent the last seventeen years in France together talking about this. It's been really dodgy financially for both of us, very difficult – terrible pressure and stress, from the recession in 1989–90 on. It made me quite surprised to realise how significant the economic factors were. I hadn't realised how much they drove me. Making work became my way of earning money. It was what I wanted to do too. I was not earning enough money, which was frustrating. It is certainly what is going on in my head now. Partly an escape from thinking about this show, which might not work because it has so many pragmatic issues…

MD: Which show?

BB: *Model Family.* Issues of funding, location, and very ambitious partners, which I like, but it's the day to day. I don't have a pension and I don't want to stop work. I have put in a business plan this year, to the Arts Council, which will potentially secure us more funding at the end of three years.[23] It's very strategic really, to find an income as an artist. It's what you have to do. I have got a whole series of new things I want to do. You have to be business savvy. I plan – so that is going to be the show for that year. And you only have the glimmerings of it, the idea behind it. Then two years or so will go into fundraising and research.

MD: If I say the word solo to you, what does it make you think of?

BB: Well it kind of depends… (She pulls a face)

MD: (Laughter) What a great face!

BB: Well, it's really odd. I have had such wonderful conversation in two days … With Adrian[24] yesterday, he said, 'so what do you think about confession?' I said, 'well actually I don't know. I have to go and get the dictionary'. I slightly object to confession like I slightly object to… I don't *object* to solo…

MD: You are allowed to object. I am interested to know what it means for you.

BB: It is because it's a definition of something, it's categorising and I always slightly want to break down categorisation, so I think that is why I wrinkle my nose up. It hadn't occurred to me that I was doing solo work. I just never looked at it like that. It never occurred to me to begin with to perform with anyone else or that there was anything 'odd' in what I was doing. Then the first time I went to the Edinburgh festival, I was in the De Marco gallery for two nights. I was quite nervous because I had never been before, and I read a review of someone's work which was really snotty. Some guy writing about a group of women's work and he said it 'smacked of the confessional'. I objected to what he said, because it was derogatory: 'women tearing their hair out on the stage' but I was also considering in my mind what that meant. Because actually if you look up the word 'confessional' in the dictionary, it is about an intimate sin and that is why it is misogynist and derogatory. So with solo – 'oh it's a solo show' and it tends to be about women and it's a weird dismissing of that work. As opposed to the 'wonderfulness' and status of being a director or working with a group of people. You brought it to my attention and I have been thinking about it. I talked to Adrian a bit yesterday about performing one to one. I don't really have any interest in doing that.

MD: Why do you like performing on your own?

BB: Because I am in control. Also I don't know how to work with other people. I want to be in control actually. I have wanted up to now to mostly be alone. I have increasingly thought about performing with other people but I couldn't quite work out their parts … I don't call my shows solo shows. I mean it is by me. I have a problem because I also dislike the word 'devised'. I can't stand it, actually. It's very theatrical whereas I come from a fine art tradition. It smacks to me of people sitting round in a studio theatre.

MD: I like to use the word 'making'.

BB: I noticed you using that. I can see why that would work. You don't say that of an artist though, do you?

MD: An artist what?

BB: A painter or sculptor – they make work. Yeah they make work. They made a piece, they made a piece. Oh yeah that's good.

MD: I am interested in what you think about the word 'solo'.

BB: When I read your questions, I thought – what is this word 'solo'? You use it a lot. I looked it up in the dictionary, because I love dictionaries. It's obviously the appropriate word. Yet is has connotations. One of the definitions is people flying on their own.

MD: Lots of things with violins.

BB: I suppose that is why it sort of surprises me every time you say it.

MD: There are other words, like monologue.

BB: I grew up with Joyce Grenfell as the only famous solo woman performing.

MD: Some people don't like the word monologue. It's dirty. You standing there talking all the time.

BB: It doesn't quite sum things up, if you are also doing other things. Monologue is more like just standing there talking, isn't it? I like it though.

MD: I like it too. I like to reclaim words. Monologue is one of them. I did a scan of recent books on devised theatre and nobody talks much about solo devising.

BB: Oh really?

MD: Well. That is a bit of a bold statement. But I think there is a whole thing about devising that comes from notion of democratic working – sharing…

BB: Which is what I find messy.

MD: With solo work, it is really not discussed in the same breath as devising and I think it is very much to do with devising in the UK coming out of a more political culture, about shared authorship and the notion that there is not just one voice or one word.

BB: That is really interesting, it is something I would certainly like to think and talk more about. Because there was always the fine line, with Pol, which was difficult for us both. I am wondering about it in relation to working with Sian – we are doing a pilot of *A Model Family* in October. We have got this Wellcome Trust money to do a pilot for this big show. How much will she contribute and is it my show? It is entirely my show. Yet it is not going to work unless it has got her own voice in it. Her view of her own family which is very different from mine. Yet that is what we said, at the very beginning of this discussion, me saying I had got back some freedom. Ownership. Authorship. Ownership of something and how you compare that to other art forms and other ways of making things. It is more simple to do things on your own and it's also exciting to work with other people.

MD: What do you think is particular about solo working?

BB: It's a bit of an unknown quantity. I am giving more talks probably now, since being at Queen Mary, to do with the mental illness, where it is just me. I haven't yet established how to go back to being entirely solo. I have the confidence in trusting my intuition back massively, and intellectual confidence. I am more confident in performing, which I learnt with Pol, and I am more relaxed about it not working. I am more confident about busking. In *Drawing on a Mother's Experience* – [the structure or form] was obvious. I get the food out in the chronological order and then I just follow the props. But what I haven't developed is an ability to know how I am going to learn to say more precise things. How do I remember it enough so I don't read it? Because if I just read it doesn't have that fluidity. I am very lazy about bothering to learn things. Giving lectures or talks – I have no sense of time. When I am performing, I have an acute sense of whether I am going on too long. Talks, I can go on forever. I don't have a sense of that discipline. I would quite like to learn that. I was giving a talk at Queen Mary's Quorum, on 'Is autobiographical work ethical?' Sian was there as we were involved with *A Model Family*. I said, 'Listen, this needs to be 45 minutes so that there is enough time for a discussion afterwards'. I did not know how to manage my time. She said, 'Look, I will give you a nod every 15 minutes'. So Sian is sitting in the front row. I talk for about 15 minutes. Apparently she started by sort of waving and I totally didn't notice her. She said when we discussed it that she would go 'urg.' I just thought it was a joke. But she had to resort to it. People said afterwards they thought someone was having a stroke. Of course what was amazing was I looked up and I saw her and I fell about laughing and I said 'Here is Sian Stevenson who I work with and she is doing this to remind me… ' and everyone laughed and relaxed because they were anxious till that point and then 15 minutes later she did it again. Again I had forgotten the time… and I said 'oh sorry'. The last time – I just about managed and it was hilarious. But I don't know how to do that entirely on my own and I want to. I want to trust my intuition and my gut feeling.

MD: What haven't I asked you?

BB: Where is the toilet?

Endnotes

1. Baker, B. & Barrett, M. 2007. *Bobby Baker: Redeeming Features of Daily Life*. London: Routledge.
2. Baker was awarded a Research Fellowship from the Arts and Humanities Research Council (AHRC) for 2005–2008, based at Queen Mary, University of London.
3. The drawings that Baker mentions in this interview become the exhibition for the Wellcome Trust in 2009, called *Bobby Baker's Diary Drawings*, and were later collected into a book *Diary Drawings: Mental Illness and Me*, published in 2010.
4. This contrasts for example with Wendy Houstoun or Nigel Charnock, who spoke of starting with physical movement, or Tim Etchells gathering written texts. Each practitioner in this book favours different kinds of core material from which the work develops.
5. The role of 'dramaturg' has tended to signify either a research role – working with scripts – or a role primarily involved with giving feedback on what has already been made. Some involvement in creating the work is part and parcel of a more contemporary role for the dramaturg: see Turner, C. & Behrndt, S.K. 2008. *Dramaturgy and Performance*. Hampshire: Palgrave Macmillan; Williams, D. 2010. 'Geographies of Requiredness: Notes on the Dramaturg in Collaborative Devising'. *Contemporary Theatre Review*, 20(20), 197–202. I write about this term – the 'contemporary dramaturg' – in relation to Baker in my Ph.D.: Dey, M. 2015. *Devising Solo Performance: A Practitioner's Enquiry*. University of Plymouth, p. 277. Available at https://pearl.plymouth.ac.uk/handle/10026.1/3289.

6. Ibid, p. 30.
7. Baker was awarded a Research Fellowship from the Arts and Humanities Research Council for 2005–2008, and was based at Queen Mary, University of London.
8. Polona Baloh Brown has been Baker's long-term collaborator, and their working relationship is discussed in more detail further on in this interview.
9. PSI is Performance Studies International – a professional association, founded in 1977, which organises events to connect academics and practitioners working in performance, including an annual performance conference held in a different country each year.
10. Aston and Harris organised a series of workshops with Lancaster University, run by women working in theatre, which culminated in their book Aston, E. & Harris, G. 2008. *Performance Practice and Process: Contemporary [Women] Practitioners*. London: Palgrave Macmillan.
11. A moment in the show, *How to Shop*. For discussion of this, see Barrett, M. in Barrett and Baker, 2007: p. 14.
12. First performed in 1988, at the ICA, London, Baker enacts an autobiographical monologue on her experiences of motherhood, drawing with food onto a large sheet, into which she winds herself, in the manner of a swiss roll, at the end of the piece.
13. In 1995, art historian and writer Marina Warner wrote an essay commissioned by the Arts Council England titled 'The Rebel at the Heart of the Joker', which is also included in Baker & Barrett 2007: pp. 95–108.
14. Ibid, p. 50.
15. *How to Shop* (1993) was a performance lecture, on the art of supermarket shopping, at Tuke Hall, Regent's College, for London International Festival of Theatre (LIFT). *Take a Peek* (1995) was an installation created at the Royal Festival Hall, South Bank Centre, London in 1995, in which the small audience go on a journey of nine funfair 'attractions' which mirror a woman's experience of visiting a health centre, performed with actors Sian Stevenson and Tamzin Griffin, at LIFT 1995. *Grown Up School* was a two-part project in which pupils, in collaboration with Baker and Marc Storer, an educationalist, created a book of their ideal school, after which Baker made an interactive show with the school children, teaching an audience of thirty adults. In *Box Story* (2001), Baker narrates ten stories from her past using ten packets of food that she paints on the floor into a map of the world. This was first performed in St Luke's Church, Holloway, London as part of LIFT 2001.
16. Baker, B. 1991–2001. *Bobby Baker: DVD Daily Life Series*. London: Arts Admin.

17. Baker, B. & Barrett, M. 2007, pp. 58, 106.
18. The name describes and frames the show – Baker starts by carrying in a very large cardboard box, containing smaller boxes of food, which she uses to construct her stories. Once the map of the world has been drawn on the floor, she ends by climbing into the original box, cutting holes in it and dancing off.
19. Dame Edna Everidge, one of the drag personas of Barry Humphries.
20. Steve Wald, the technical director.
21. Jocelyn Pook, music composer.
22. Andrew Whittuck, whom Baker was married to at the time of interview and who photographed much of her work.
23. Baker's company, Daily Life Ltd., became a National Portfolio funded company by the Arts Council in 2012.
24. Adrian Howells, writer and performer. He was interviewing Baker as part of his own research work in Glasgow.

Mike Pearson

Deaf Birds, Late Snow (1978) ©Steve Allison

Mike Pearson is a relentlessly self-challenging performance maker, writer and academic. He has been experimenting and stretching the boundaries of what performance is and can be ever since he joined physical theatre company RAT Theatre in 1972, and then in 1974 founded Cardiff Laboratory for Theatrical Research, which later became Cardiff Laboratory Theatre. His early training in archaeology is everywhere manifest in the layered, multi-disciplinary approach he brings to making and writing about performance and his incorporation of history, geography and landscape into his works. He is perhaps most widely known for his large-scale site-specific theatre work with Welsh company Brith Gof, which he founded with Lis Hughes Jones in 1981, working in abandoned

ship docks and train depots, using v[...]
sitions in which performers played j[...]
mance events. Solo working is perh[...]
to mind from this kind of legacy. H[...]
view is that over the years, Pearson h[...]
a considerable number of solo piece[...]
he returns again and again, a realisat[...]

"Familiars": things we recognize

He discusses all his performed so[...]
Cardiff Laboratory for Theatrical F[...]
1974 to the audio walk *Carrlands* in 2007 – thirty years of solo making.
Out of all my interviewees, he most challenged my attempts to 'define'
solo working. He offered for discussion a variety of configurations in how
he made and performed his work. This included being directed by others
but devising alone (*The Lesson in Anatomy*, 1974); devising and performing alone (*Deaf Birds, Late Snow*, 1978; *Whose Idea Was The Wind*, 1978;
From Memory, 1991; *Bubbling Tom*, 2000); co-devising (with designer
Mike Brookes) but performing alone (*Dead Men's Shoes*, 1997; *The first
five miles*, 1998); devising alone and then performing with someone else
(with saxophonist Peter Brötzmann, who improvises freely alongside
him, in a separate yet shared performance space).

Like other interviewees, he also spoke of collaborating with other
experts on specific parts of his performed solos (*Bubbling Tom*; *Carrlands*).
The above range helped me further understand what I considered a
'must' or defining feature that made solo 'solo' – namely that the vision
or concept of the work is one person's, although others can be involved
in a myriad of ways.[1]

Pearson's solo work contrasts with his spectacular, large-scale, somewhat
impersonal physical theatre. It is small scale, finely detailed, built around
particular objects and multi layered spoken texts. In 1992, while including personal autobiographical material was common in solo work (the
self as source and life narratives abound in solo performance art), including actual recorded words from other people was a relatively new practice, outside documentary or verbatim theatre. This is pre-social media,
reality television and widely accessible mobile technology. He offers a
clear sense of a strong family culture while also broadening the work out
to find resonance in and with his audience. He also speaks evocatively

about 'familiars', the term he uses to refer to people, objects, and patterns of behaviour, which can accompany him and others in their work.

Mike clearly relishes challenge and admires endurance – for example, making himself learn very long, extended monologues; rehearsing saxophone playing in public only to realise he is not good enough to play it in performance; taking on the British weather and losing; and inviting gossip and dialogue with an audience who speak over him. Along with other interviewees in this book, he plays with the stereotype of the soloist who displays their skills in a virtuosic manner (a practice he nonetheless much admires in others) and instead reveals an altogether more flawed human individual who has to struggle and to do battle to even reach the end of the work. In regarding his solos chronologically, it became evident how one piece raises questions that the next piece engages with – performance research which both fulfils funding criteria but is also clearly the result of Pearson's continuous curiosity and refusal to repeat previous formulas or formats.

A precise compositional sensibility is evident in his solo making and forms the essential scaffolding around which he creates performance material. His sense of structure, in making, composition and improvisation is everywhere present. Not for him the use of an 'outside eye' – in fact he provocatively suggests this notion of 'externality' in terms of composition creates a work seen backwards. His own vision is foremost, while he also has great enthusiasm for others' work, giving numerous detailed examples of solo moments he admires. This speaks of a solo performer well attuned to the skills of others.

Performance Chronology

Mike Pearson's first solo work was in 1974, in *Flesh* and *Asylum*, two sections of *The Lesson in Anatomy* performed in the Sherman Arena Theatre, Cardiff, and that launched Cardiff Laboratory for Theatrical Research. He then went on to make two small solo pieces about birds in 1978 – *Whose Idea Was The Wind* and *Deaf Birds, Late Snow* performed at Chapter Arts Centre, Cardiff. In 1981, he co-founded and became joint artistic director of Brith Gof and went on to make a number of highly successful large-scale site-specific performances with the company. He returned to solo making in 1991, with a trilogy of autobiographical solo works first performed at the Welsh Folk Museum in St Fagan's, Cardiff, and collectively called *From Memory*, including *A Death in the Family*, *Patagonia*, and later – following its substitution for an original unnamed third part – *The Body of Evidence* (1995), the latter reworked into the piece *Blood* (sometimes also titled *Autopsy*) with Mike Brookes in 1998 and performed in Cardiff docklands. His collaborative relationship with Brookes continued in a [...] f works which they co-devised; Pearson working on th[...] performing solo and Brookes involved in [...] al scenography. These pieces included [...] d at the Welsh Industrial and Maritime [...] *les...* (1998), performed outdoors at [...] ystwyth)[2]; and *The man who ate his* [...] Castle Theatre in Aberystwyth. In [...] obiographical guided walk around H[...] d village, which lived on by being lat[...] Dee Heddon in 2002 and subsequently aga[...] a group of students from Manchester University.[3] His [...] *Carrlands*, in the Ancholme valley in Lincolnshire and made at the time of this interview in 2007, is the last solo discussed here in detail. After this interview, in 2008, Pearson created another audio walk, *Winter*, for Groenweld Castle, Baarn, in the Netherlands and went on to recreate his solos from *The Lesson in Anatomy* in the Sherman Theatre on 5 July 2014, forty years to the day from its original staging.

[Handwritten note: The responsibility falls on the spectator — very interesting / Audience as part-performer]

The Interview

MD: Are you working on anything solo at the moment?

MP: I am. It's of a strange kind. I have got a small research grant to create three audio walks for a particular landscape in North Lincolnshire, the area where I was brought up. The idea is to create three one-hour texts, which then integrate music and sampling from original interviews that I did; so it's a fairly big writing project. Each of the hours is divided into four fifteen-minute movements. What I have been trying to do is to find a way of speaking, because the idea is that these would be available as mp3 files to download. We will make some physical copies for older citizens but basically the idea is you can download them and take them and listen to them on site, on an iPod under whatever conditions the listener–spectator wants.[4] So if you want to go when it is pouring with rain or in the middle of the night, you can; instead of all that endless trauma – 'Is it going to rain or not?' – with site work, the responsibility transfers to the spectator. It is a performance work because of the way I speak the text, which I have worked long and hard on. But it also has to address every single person who would ever want to listen to it, which is actually quite different from pieces of solo or theatre work where you are quite certain who your audience is going to be, and you build it around that presupposition. To make work for anybody is a big challenge in the writing, but also in the speaking. One of the ambitions in the writing is to mix up quite detailed information about the places with instructions to the listener, so that the listener becomes part-performer in the role. You can't do that by saying – 'Now lift your leg up and jump about' – it's not that, but by trying to imagine things for the participant. What I hope they begin to do is create imaginary pictures in this landscape, which is actually very flat, agricultural and unforgiving.

MD: Where is it exactly?

MP: It's a river called the Ancholme in North Lincolnshire. It runs into the Humber and since the 1820s it has been a more or less a straight-cut sewer. The old river has been completely canalised. It winds around the canal and emerges either side sometimes; basically it is a manmade land-scape and although it looks like very benign, agricultural land, there is an incredible effort that goes on to keep it like that. If ever there is a high tide in the Humber and they can't let the sluice open to let the water out – if ever there are heavy thunderstorms and high tide – that is when it gets really dangerous. I think eventually somebody will say it's no longer worth the effort. All along the east coast there are similar kinds of floodplains.

MD: So just to clarify. There are four fifteen-minute sections?

MP: For each of three different locations down the valley. I would expect most people to download an hour and then go and do that whole hour. I am working with John Hardy, the composer.[5] I did a lot of local interviews with farmers and ornithologists and so on. One idea we have is to try and 'ghost-in' odd phrases or things that people say to me into the soundtrack.

MD: Are those the interviews you mentioned earlier on?

MP: Yes. That has been a year-long project. I have spent time in the field, talking to people. John and I have walked those landscapes. Now it is all coming to a head. Over the summer the hard work begins. I have recorded two of the hour-long sections already. I am doing the third one tomorrow. Then John is going to start the composition work against the texts. So in one way my job as a performer was fairly straightforward. It won't be modified by John although we may cut it slightly.

MD: When you said you had to work really hard, that is because your body is not there, isn't it? You are only a voice.

MP: Absolutely, all of those things as a performer one would rely on – presence… How do you make yourself present in absence? Now I know that that is probably fairly familiar to actors who do radio and who do audio recordings of famous novels, but it is a bit different in our field. I do appreciate there is a lot of work that uses collages but I think this one is slightly different. It is like a combination of one of these things that you would get at a National Trust property, perhaps, but a more dramatic approach. I have been not only in the field with local people but also with so-called disciplinary experts. I had two days, one with archaeologists, one with geographers, and they were absolutely delighted, because they were almost framed like classic field trips, which geographers don't do much anymore. Two blokes wandering about in a landscape talking about how this came to be like this. But talking to the archaeologist about this was really interesting – John Barrett, who is an old college friend of mine and who is now a Professor at Sheffield University. He is on the committee that is considering what to do with Stonehenge. Not only in terms of what to do with the roads – what to do physically there and that is a matter of endless discussion – but how to interpret the place for the visitor. They have begun to realise that for almost everybody, there is a very, very low threshold for remembering data. Even I, as a kind of archaeologist, couldn't tell you the particular phases at Stonehenge, off the top of my head, with the dates. If that is the first thing you tell a visitor, they get frustrated because they can't remember it and then they begin to think they are stupid and the whole visit becomes totally unsatisfactory. So what they are thinking of doing is reversing that completely. Trying to provide the visitor with interpretive tools – 'Think about this; What do you think this may or may not be? How did this happen? If you were given this, how might that be?' I was very taken by that and I have tried to do that in the audio works, really helping the visitor.

MD: I once went for a job in a museum and it was similar – how do you provide access to people and show them things rather than put them in glass boxes.

MP: Exactly. Because John is a Neolithic expert he is often dealing with monumentality. So actually when you are looking at Stonehenge you are always looking at the *thing* and I guess the challenge for this project of mine is that you are not looking at anything in particular and indeed you are so low down you are not getting any perspective at all. What are you looking at, in close up, and what is the experience of walking down a straight canal?

MD: He is one of your collaborators? What was he offering you?

MP: Well, what I have talked about above and also whether one can move beyond the monumental and talk about process. How did this place come into being? He had a beautiful notion. These are drained marshlands; they are not that much different from Glastonbury. It's just that the past is very deeply buried, in an incredible plenitude because it was a wet landscape. Just occasionally, in the bottom of a river when they are dredging, they pull out a Bronze Age longboat. You have this notion of a blanket of history that this veneer of agriculture is sitting on top of. That was quite resonant for me. I walked all day, with him, and with the geographers [too], and visited various sites and I recorded a conversation exactly like this, sitting in my car, because that was the most convenient place to do it. But parked up, in that classic English way of sitting in a car, a couple looking at nothing in particular, with your tea, and just talking about what we were looking at. It was one of the geographers who said it was like a gazebo. It's been a very convenient project because it is something that I have been able to do a little bit of, almost daily, in terms of writing. Although it is a year-long project and we have a deadline for delivery, it doesn't quite have that pressure of 'your performance is in three weeks time', so the process of doing it has been much more drawn out. It has included the interview process, conventional library research, field visits and regular conversations with John Hardy that have been really helpful; and then thinking about what, or how, I am going to approach it. Listening to a certain range of contemporary composers so I might have something to contribute…

MD: Did you say what the source for the project was? How did it start?

MP: It's a kind of projection of the performative that emerges from *Theatre/Archaeology*. (It is exactly the same process I talk about in the book *In Comes I*; one or two places that I mention in the book are actually the places that the audio works address.) In *Theatre Archaeology*, Michael Shanks and I talk about *deep mapping* and how you can build some appreciation of historical narrative depth in a particular place, and I wanted to do further work in the area. That was one thing. I am keen to be led back there quite often, because most of my correspondents including my mum are very aged and infirm now. So there is a sense that I am doing this for and with them. My dad's cousin, Kath, who is now 86, she is the only person living who actually lived on the river. They had one of the very few houses built on the riverbank. One of the fifteen-minute movements is her story, which is extraordinary. It was so interesting to work on. What do you say? What questions do you ask people? You cannot say 'What was it like?' because it is just too general. In the questioning, I talked to lots of different local people, particularly older people. There are one or two keys that are very helpful. The most helpful was, 'So what was it like in the winter of 1947?' which was the worst winter in the twentieth century. People go 'Oh my God'; Kath tells this fantastic story of the river completely freezing and German and Italian prisoners of war who worked on their farm playing soccer on the ice. Very nice images. But then it melted and there was serious risk of it flooding – the river broke up into icebergs, so these enormous lumps of ice floated by and her dad had to stand in the window of one of their houses with a big pole trying to keep ice from smashing into it.

If you look at it, it's a completely benign, undifferentiated agricultural landscape. But if you can then put that image (of icebergs) into the mind of a visitor–spectator, while they are standing at that spot, while they are in that locality, then that's the ambition. There are quite a lot of anecdotes like that, and the farmers are great. The other question I ask everybody who lived or worked on the land is, 'So did you find any bog oak?' 'Oh we found this tree once that was fifteen yards long.' My dad's cousin said, 'When we were ploughing we used to have a wooden peg between the plough and the tractor so that if the ploughshare hit a bog oak this wooden peg would snap, instead of completely buckling the ploughshare'. They are finding wood that is harder than a metal ploughshare. The farmers were telling me that on some fields there is a floor of prehistoric fallen bog oak. Just like a floor under the landscape.

MD: Incredible. I have never heard of bog oak.

MP: It's close to swearing – 'bog oak'. Lots of non-conformists, the Primitive Methodist farmers call it 'carr oak'. That is the title of the project *Carrlands* – these very flat lands near the river are called 'carrs' in North Lincolnshire. These wetlands were formed around 5,000 BC. They became forested with oak and alder, almost impenetrable, big wet forests. When they fell, the water wasn't going away, so they formed mires. Really classic bog. They must be more like the swamps in Florida. That is the impression. This oak, when it fell, in those waterlogged conditions there is a process that goes on and I am not sure of it but actually the wood gets harder and almost fossilises. You can't cut it. I remember taking lumps to school to try and use in art classes. You couldn't saw it. My father worked for the Potato Marketing Board. He was a fieldsman. He spent all day looking at potatoes and talking to farmers, so laying his hands on some bog oak was not a problem for him.

MD: I have no chronology of your solo work. Can you tell me it?

MP: Almost the very first thing we did, with Cardiff Laboratory for Theatrical Research, in 1974 was called *The Lesson in Anatomy*, based on [Antonin] Artaud's texts and directed by two French directors. It was four solos, of which I did two. The first one we called *Flesh*, which was Artaud's writing on the body physical; and I [also] did the fourth one, which was the social body, particularly his asylum experiences. I remember when they arrived they said they had some things they wanted me to do. They brought Denis Diderot's *Encyclopaedia*. They wanted me to get a whole set of those things that dentist put on your teeth, those things with screws on. They wanted me to walk out with all of those on. They also wanted a marble slab – an autopsy slab to perform on. It was quite interesting because none of that was available to us. Marble slabs had absolutely disappeared from any medical work at all, because bacteria gather in the cracks and crevices. So a friend made a beautiful white table, really thick. I worked on that and I decided none of this [dental apparatus] was going to work. So what I did was I got a dinner suit; that was it – black trousers and a jacket. For *Flesh*, I decided that I would only use that – the table and the suit. It taught me an enormous amount about solo work – not only about the process of creating it. Working with the table, I was thinking 'How can I be on the table, how can I be adjacent to the table, how can bits of me get put on the table and not other bits? If I use the suit how can I create images where bits of me are exposed and bits of me covered up? Because I am not very confident about the text, what could happen with the suit? Oh – I will read it off the label in the inside jacket pocket. I will have it on a matchbox that I take out and play with'. Working with all kinds of strategies of devising... Then what was great about the show was that it was in the Arena Theatre in the Sherman,[6] which was a three-quarter circle with the table in the middle like an operating theatre, like a medical situation. That relationship between me and the audience was prefigured by the seating: I could be a specimen, I could be a lecturer, I could fuse all of those things one to another, because the scenographic concept had that written in it. That really taught me a lot – 'I can address the audience directly now and I can do it in the guise of that person or that person because that goes with this situation'. That was very instructive.

MD: And you devised that.

MP: And I devised that, with the directors. But they left me to it; at the end of every day they would come in to see what I had done. Some days they would come in and I would start and they would just walk out. After ten seconds they would walk out. That was really hard, hard...

MD: (Laughter) What sort of directing was that?

MP: Well it was, 'We will know it when we see it and you have to work your socks off to get to this point. We are not going to tell you how to do it'. Which was great. In this same piece I also did this last solo, in a shirt and trousers. The *Flesh* piece was all about hard physical work. What I had to try and do by the second solo, which came half an hour later, was that I had to completely dissolve all that physicality, in order to be completely soft, completely compliant. Within the space of a show having to create a different kind of physicality and I developed this way of doing it – lying on the floor backstage and I used to shake; really, really shaking, trying to get rid of all that tension of that performance and that thing I had just done. How do you strip all that out and then be in a very calm, weak, quiet place and still keep some kind of presence in front of an audience?

MD: Because you were being what?

Whose Idea was the Wind (1978) ©Steve Allison

MP: Because most of the texts I chose were the post electro-shock texts. I was still likely to rage in any one moment, but the physical effect, I had to somehow represent. It was a very formative experience and terrific – the tw[...]

Handwritten note: Don't like "will never have that skill", Don't want to put money, time & effort in that skill

MD: I [...] experience before that?

MP: Y[...] we had had the student group before [...] how in which we kicked [what later b[...] off as a professional entity. It was th[...] or three things with Cardiff Lab. d[...]. Solo because I suppose it was somet[...]ng I did not want to impose [...] nybody else. There were two pieces [...] as a tiny show, *Whose Idea Was The Wind*, made in 1977 or 1978. I did it on the top of a table, with an audience sitting really close, just with my hands on the table. I used bird skulls and bits of birds' wings and feathers and I managed to find a way of supporting them in my hands, so I could create these strange crows, just with my hands. I used a series of stories about birds, mainly from Native American and Inuit poems and traditions. You could only see my head and my hands; and it was just lit on the table. A lot of people remember that little show. Maybe that was the start of… because most of the work I did and people knew I was interested in was quite hard physical stuff. Suddenly to do something based on storytelling or that kind of narrative, it seemed quite atypical. I can't ever imagine learning play texts [though]. You say something and then I say something… aagh. But I found I had no problem remembering long blocks of text.

MD: Like in *Bubbling Tom*.

MP: Yes – exactly. Maybe that was the start of that background storytelling thing. Then the other solo show I made, which was a bit more theatrical – sorry, I mean 'me moving around in space' – was called *Deaf Birds* and again it was using a similar kind of material. I didn't really know what I was doing but again, I was using a lot of the bird material. One of the interesting things that I did in that work was I played solo saxophone. I am a terrible saxophone player and I said I will play the saxophone in this – I had a soprano saxophone. One of the young guys that was associated with Cardiff Lab., who lived in Oxford, wrote half a dozen short motif pieces for me.

MD: Why did you say to yourself, 'I am going to play the saxophone?'

MP: Because with solo work, to challenge yourself in that way was always a thing. Maybe the challenge with *Deaf Birds* was to try and speak texts, to tell the story *and* put these musical pieces into the work. He sent me the scores and I worked on them; and then again, in terms of process, he did a really interesting thing. He asked me to go to Oxford and spend the day there and whenever he told me to play the pieces, I had to play the pieces. So I arrived and he took me into a church and he said, 'Play the pieces'. We walked down the High Street, we were outside Woolworths[7] and he said, 'Play the pieces'. We went into this building and he said, 'Walk through that door and play the pieces'. I walked through the door and I am on this stage of the Sheldonian,[8] the oldest public music hall in the world. I was awful and again it was very instructive, liberating actually, because what you may or may not do in performance, suddenly when you had to do that in a public arena for people who don't even know they are an audience. I remember the Woolworths' experience very well, because I got moved on.

MD: What did that experience do?

MP: In a kind of negative way, it made me appreciate the skill required for musical performance and that I was never going to have that skill. So I will never attempt to do it again. But also, it's about having that absolute responsibility for delivering. There is nothing else, just you and that thing to be delivered. If it is appalling then the only person you have to blame, in a way, is you. So those two pieces linked together. They were in the background, in Cardiff Lab.

Then I didn't do any solo work in the early days of Brith Gof. I didn't have the impulse to do it. We made the series of big works – *Gododdin, Pax, Haearn*.[9] And it was about the time of *Haearn* I began to get very uneasy about what was happening to me in the big works, but also what we were doing with performers – because they were at such a scale and involved so many different elements. Performers assume more often than not that they are carrying the meaning in a theatrical way. Well, in those big shows that was certainly not the case. The physical performers were only ever part of the architecture of the piece. In any one moment the music might have been carrying the emotive meaning, not the performers. The audience might be looking at the band, not the performers.

As a strategy to recover something for myself, I started to think about solo works again. Also there were one or two events, which also made me want to do something particular. The main thing was my father's death. He never ever saw me perform. He just wouldn't acknowledge that [I performed]. It wasn't talked about it in the family; it was like I had gone to sea. It's not a disappointment to me, it was just one of those things that happened. I started work on something that actually became a trilogy. The first piece was called *From Memory*[10] and was about the death of my father, and family. I began to realise that within the family we had a very long tradition of family gossip because my grandma and granddad kept the village chip shop and taxi service. There was this incredible flow-through of information in my early life. I began to wonder whether one could capture a way of speaking or telling that was not much more than *that* kind of speaking. It was quite low key but told very personal things that you wouldn't perhaps expect to hear in a theatrical context. Now this is all very familiar, but in 1992, autobiographical work [was less so]. I wanted to make some of those experiences a bit more evident, to talk about things like the rural working-class experience, which we often hear little about except in some bucolic romantic manner… *From Memory* establishes, in 1992, all of the techniques I think that I was able to extend and play with in *Bubbling Tom*. The most important thing is that I included very different orders of text: personal; revelatory; the description of an event (my mother seeing my father's body); a poem by Thomas Hardy (which is never introduced as 'and here is Thomas Hardy') so there is that kind of seamlessness of text. There is a comic moment, about my ears, and also a superstitious moment – my grandmother talking about touching a dead body, and so on and so on. All of that kind of mixing, being able to put found poetic text in the framework was important to me. It gave me the confidence to believe that material that was in essence autobiographical could still be opened out. Even though I was talking about real details of personal experience, of family life, I could find a way of doing it that would have a resonance for an audience…

I was aware early on then about how texts operate with and against each other and how in selecting and ordering and composing them you can make an audience come and go with you. It is like you are whispering something quite private in their ear. Then in the next moment you pull back into talking about the repercussions of heart attacks, or you can do the Thomas Hardy poetic section. In that way, you are working with the intimately familiar and the infinitely strange. Even if you are working with very personal material, you have to find those moments that an audience can identify with. I don't necessarily mean that they have the same experience, or whatever, but that [they] are identifiable. Then moments that make you and your family so peculiar, that it is unimaginable.

I began to appreciate how solo performance allows you to put anything next to anything. There is a coherence simply because there is one person doing it. That was a big revelation… A seamlessness began to develop which was helpful – the writing process became the learning process as well. And again that might not be entirely apparent to people – that there are not distinct processes going on there. When you are writing you are already imagining saying these things, which is quite different from a playwright. You are already writing certain registers or tonal things into the text. You are writing it to be spoken or to be performed, so not necessarily thinking about its literary qualities and because you are involved with the text at that level, then learning it doesn't become another process – you are already halfway committed.

MD: For you, perhaps. For me, I use a lot of writing but then I have to learn it. I let go of it and when I come back to it, it's a different thing. It doesn't stay the same for me.

MP: But that is interesting. I am not sure I am very good at acting and certainly not very good at learning text in that way… So *From Memory* became a trilogy and the very first staging of it was in the [reconstructed, circular] cockpit in the Welsh Folk Museum in St Fagans, Cardiff. It was site work in a completely different kind of a site. But actually being in that quasi-performative situation was really helpful. The space was enclosed, so you can see everyone, you can see how far you are going to need to speak to reach them and there was this little performing area in the middle if you choose to use it. Because of that setup, I had a place where I could sit which was just basically within the circle of audience and I could also go into the middle, into this little cockpit if I so chose. So again, spatially there was a way of articulating the material. Whereas if I had been in a theatre space from the outset that would have led to another thing. The space, in retrospect, was important – there was a basic spatial structure about the piece.

MD: Did you choose that context, or was it given to you, or happenstance?

MP: It was happenstance, though I did have good contacts [with the Museum] at that time and we had done Brith Gof work there before.[11] The cockpit was this place that people would look at when they go to St Fagans, but because they can't show any pictures of chickens fighting chickens, it's a 'So what went on here?'…. Whereas [if it had been set] in a 1930s or 1940s house, people would go, 'Oh look at that, we had one of those, we had one of those'. So this was really performative, it had that performative potency built into it. I did that there and I began to then wonder whether one could transfer that way of talking and performing into material that was far less personal. How would it be if you could keep that going?

MD: The style – the mode?

MP: Yeah exactly, to give data that was very personal, but from a subject matter that wasn't biographical. And because the first one was about my father's death, I thought 'What about other deaths'? The second one I made [was] about the shooting of Llwyd ap Iwan in Patagonia in 1909. It's a long story but probably he was shot by Butch Cassidy and the Sundance Kid. It was one of these classic Welsh moments in Patagonia and a completely different kind of thing; and I wore a mask and coat and I had guns… I quite liked the idea of doing a Western. We don't have enough of these genres in theatre anymore; we should get back to the Western. Then the third one [in the *From Memory* trilogy] – at that time I did a very, very unsatisfactory work because I didn't have the real key to it and it involved me cooking chips. It was trying to be a family thing again and it just never worked. I don't think I performed it more than once in the trilogy. So I began to work on another final piece,[12] which eventually had a life beyond the initial impulse. It was simple – and I had to be very careful talking about it. But it was about the murder of a young Cardiff woman, a prostitute named Lynette White; she was murdered

in the house opposite where our office was in Cardiff docks. It was clear
from the outset that a single white man had killed her and so of course,
true to form, South Wales Police arrested five black men and they became
the Cardiff Five and then the Cardiff Three. Two things happened in all
of that – she herself disappeared from the story, and it became a story
about other things. It became a story about old Cardiff and new Cardiff
and how quickly we wanted to get rid of that world and how shiny and
bright new Cardiff now is. I wanted to recover her story. The other thing
is that she was killed on Valentine's Day 1988, when we [Brith Gof] were
actually there. South Wales Police didn't have a clue, so they decided to
do one of the earliest experiments of DNA testing. They tested us all. The
only way they could think to do it was to take the point of the scene of
crime and then to work out like this – DNA testing men in a fifty-yard
radius. They came round and said, 'Would you be willing' and we said,
'Yes of course'. But at that time there was no swabbing or anything. I had
to go and give blood in a police station. It had very strange things about
it indeed. Anyway, I made a piece about that and it became the third
part of the trilogy. It was during the Lynette piece that I discovered I had
the ability, strangely, that I didn't know I had, to remember long, long
bodies of [non-biographical] text, particularly if I had written them. It
wasn't like I had to work out a voicing for them because there was already
a voice there in the writing. So the process of writing became important
within the whole theatrical process.[13]

MD: Do you have common strategies for making your solo work?

MP: In the earlier work the struggle was always to find a physical coherence and logic; that was the nature of the work and youth in general
and we shouldn't dismiss that. What one is doing is building one action
or one physical thing onto another; a building process of 'How do I get
from that to that. How does that articulate *against* that?' If I look at the
earlier work, the only way I could do this was – I am not dance-trained
in that way – with objects. 'How do I work with a table, how do I work
with this suit, how do I work if I have got these six bird skulls?'

Actually, I had to have a companion. What is the thing that is accom-
panying you in the physical work? Maybe all of those things become
familiars to start to build things round. I have talked to archaeologists

about it, about the investment that performers put into objects. We talked about what happens if you lose those familiars or break them, because that can be very traumatic.

MD: Can you say more about the subject of familiars?

MP: I wonder whether there are within the solo performances certain thematics. Or whether there are certain ways of talking about things that [also] become familiars. They may be quite transitory, quite momentary… I don't mean they are long things. It might be a mention of a specific person in solo work or a particular attitude to revelatory material or indeed the revelatory material itself. Whether you are telling a secret. The untold. That might be a familiar.

MD: What is the difference between that and say a habit. Or a reflex. Your 'habit', one might say, is to work with challenges, for example.

MP: Yes. Hm. I do have habits. I don't know really.

MD: The word is so evocative – 'familiar'.

MP: Yeah, maybe what I was thinking about in that is that within solo performance, you have these illusionary others with you. So you populate the work with these other people.

MD: You do that?

MP: I definitely do that with the autobiographical material.

MD: Using memory?

MP: Yes – memory. If you can work that, it can seem like a crowd with you, as opposed to just you.

MD: Are you also saying that one of the alternatives to physical composing is to have objects which suggest narratives or accompany you?

MP: It varies, because as soon as you involve objects you do engage in forms of advanced play. How to resist 'a thousand and one things to do with a bucket'? Even in the earlier work there was some kind of conceptual process going on through the object. What would happen if I used a table? Now I have got the table, what am I going to do with it?

MD: I also get a strong sense of an ordering process in your work. Even in your improvised work with Peter Brötzmann, you go with some objects,[14] and in *Bubbling Tom*, you clearly conceptualise the work and the frame beforehand.

MP: Maybe it's because of my history. I do need fairly formal structures in place, I have to say.

MD: When you say your 'history', what do you mean exactly?

MP: Because I am not trained. I do not have that facility to improvise freely. Though interestingly when I think back, some of the work that Richard Gough and I did in the mid-1970s, it was extremely free in its articulation, even in front of audiences.[15] But I have increasingly needed a certain formality – partly expediency, certainly in the 1980s and then after the fall of Brith Gof in the 1990s. I think concept and structure were the things that we had in place of money. We did not have the wherewithal, like Odin [Teatret], to rehearse for a year. We had to train

Bubbling Tom (2000) ©Hugo Glendinning

ourselves to work on a more conceptual, framing level, without necessarily enacting anything. Then, when it came to the moment of enacting it, at least we had those structures to work within…

… And then of course, I, of my own volition, started to make other solo works, the main one being *Bubbling Tom*, the impetus for which came from several different directions. It was the year I was fifty, so I wanted to do something for me. My mum had never seen me perform and also it was an opportunity. Forced Entertainment and Live Art Agency[16] advertised this 'Small Acts of the Millennium' scheme; I made a proposal and I got about £2,000. They had these relatively small amounts of money, so I decided I would try and make something in Hibaldstow. Again, all of the attendant information about the context I suppose skewed the way that the work eventually turned out. I knew my mum would be there, so perhaps not talking about the death of my father would be a good thing. The villagers might be there, so I might not want to say certain things about certain events in the past. I don't mean censorship – it was sensitivity to context. I had no idea whether anybody would come from the outside at all, even though we did advertise it. I assumed my audience would be a village audience and I pitched it accordingly. I made sure that I could embrace the largest number of people who might show up. Of course, banging on about family matters for two hours was not going to be helpful. So I always had to push it out, even though when I look at the writing or the performance of it, I think there was some moments where, if I say something that only three people in the audience would understand, actually I quite appreciated that. Maybe you can make a text in a performance where there are various layers of understanding about what is being said. You never exclude anyone, but there are moments of real personal resonance. The work on it was through a process that has become quite familiar now, of talking to family and talking to people who knew me when I was that age. I interviewed my schoolteacher from when I was seven, Marion; she was in the audience. I decided to do a guided tour of the landscape I knew at the age of seven. I was constantly drawn to what had changed, what was the same, why it had changed and so on. Then thinking about anecdotes from the past, some of which I thought people in the audience would definitely remember, others that they would not, because they happened to me while they were doing something else in the village.

MD: I enjoyed very much the moment in the story of the woman in the choir who always sings one note – and when you said that you paused and three or four people in the audience chorused with you – she always sings one note *behind.*

MP: Exactly. All of those things, like looking at photographs of myself and then relocating myself in those places, which are now completely new or on other scale… In the later work, the writing process is really important, so that by the time I come to physicalising, making [it] in front of an audience, there is something that is really carrying me. It's like a support mechanism. What I get is a buzzing voice in my head, which is the tone that this thing is going to have. However disparate the material appears to be, I know it is going to come down to a particular kind of voicing. I might not speak it but I think that that voice begins to happen in my head and the material begins to pile in… So, constructing, voicing, and then thinking, 'How am I going to place all of that, how am I going to voice that, spatially'? Because again in *Bubbling Tom*, the physical rhetorics are quite low key… So, I wave my arms around a lot, as I have been doing throughout while talking to you; I do that naturally. On one or two occasions I imitate people. But I didn't want to make them into grotesques. I just give the audience enough so they go, 'Oh yeah – Oh yeah'… With *Bubbling Tom*, I learnt this big text but I never rehearsed it on the street. Well, actually I did walk around very quietly, but of course in a village everyone knows you are doing it. You can't do this incognito. I had to be quite explicit with people about what I was doing. What I had to have in place were a certain number of things that would get me through the performance. I had in mind some physical things that I might do and the text [that] was absolutely embedded. What I hadn't anticipated in performance was that people would a) constantly interrupt me and b) start talking the moment I stopped talking. Your work then becomes a mnemonic for their past. But when that happens, you can't hold on to the dynamic, or you have to work very tactically to regain [it], when you want to make a point.

MD: Who do you collaborate with?

MP: I have to say I don't think I have ever been in a situation where, making solo work, I have felt the desire to refer to an outside eye. In almost everything that I have done, whether physical or narrative, I am always looking for an internal logic. Whatever the work is like, it has to really hang together internally from my point of view. Having an outside eye would be for me like looking in a mirror, so you would get it all backwards anyway. I don't think I have ever asked, 'How does it seem from the outside?' Whether it works, or not, is another matter, but for me it has always had to have that internal logic and you only find that... the performer has to find that themselves.

MD: So you are speaking about collaboration which uses an 'outside eye', a person who might give you feedback and whether you need them or not. You also spoke about working with experts, archaeologists and curators and Mike Brookes[17] as other kinds of collaborator. I guess you do think of other people as your collaborators?

MP: Well Mike, clearly, in particular. But I do think there is an age thing. With younger collaborators there is always some kind of deference – whether you want it or not – around the fact that you are aged and you must therefore be more experienced and you must have all kinds of things to say about whether this is right or wrong. It's an interesting question...

MD: What's interesting about it?

MP: Well, what is this thing we call collaboration? What are you expecting of the person you are working with? Maybe I will start with the most recent and work backwards. I decided to create three solo works in Chapter in November [2007]. I am going to go back to big blocks of textual material and see if I can still work them. On a level where the physical performance is quite pulled back. I am going to be fifty-nine by then. I am going to do three hour-long shows, maybe longer than an hour. We are going to call it *Three Welsh Landscapes*, and the first one is about the Beardmore Glacier in Antarctica. That is where Edgar Evans, the fifth man on Scott's expedition, died.

MD: He was the Welshman who got blamed for it?

MP: Yes. The second is Nant y Pysgod in Patagonia. The third is Mynydd Bach in Ceredigion – which is [about] The War of the Little Englishman. I am almost there with writing the text. But Chapter is going to be undergoing renovation. It's already started. The theatre is out of commission. The theatre programmer there said, 'Why don't you try doing something in the old dance studio?' It's just an empty room. It's not much different from when it was a classroom. It has got windows all around. It's quite small. It has only got one door, so I am sure the audience is going to be limited anyway – thirty or forty people in there. Mike is going to work for a fortnight on this. I said to him – 'Well I would really like to do these three texts and we've got this room. That is it'. 'Well', he said almost immediately, 'I think I am going to put all of the technology outside the room'. He has the idea of building scaffolding towers and putting the lighting through the windows. I said 'Good, great'. So to answer your question then. My fascination is where that decision comes from and how we can agree on it immediately. Now I know he has probably been harbouring that desire for a long time and then opportunity comes along. But I think it comes from mutual respect. I don't think it is a shared aesthetic, because we [don't] have that. We are sensitive to the things we respectively do. But I am not sure we ever come to a situation completely empty. That is one thing. We do very often talk quite a lot without it necessarily ever feeling that we were in some kind of third place that was only made from the two of us… When you talk about collaboration you almost imagine that there is this special state of collaborating. I am not sure we ever get into that state. Again it is always pragmatically related to the problem or brief at hand. The worst situations are those I have been in where you have arranged to collaborate with somebody and you think, 'What are we all doing in this room?'

MD: It is interesting to me, hearing your language and the way you talk, you talk very musically. You talk about voicing and buzz and you talk about sound and now you are talking about timing, in a way.

MP: Well, funny you should mention that. I am not a frustrated musician, but I do actually find that [I use a] compositional way of thinking about things. Maybe that has been there from early on. I do see the piece as a composition, whether it be solo work or whatever kind. I need to know the shape of the whole thing; I need to know the components within the whole thing. I do feel awkward about just setting out and letting it unwind in whatever way it will. I am aware of wanting to draw the whole thing into some kind of composition, which of course is very difficult when you are working with Peter [Brötzmann]. Because Peter will play until someone tells him to stop playing, or he falls over. And so, I say, 'We might stop now', which is an interesting moment…

MD: If I say the word solo to you, what do you imagine?

MP: The best and the worst probably – almost simultaneously. Incredibly accomplished work, where the solo artist is so in control of the material, so centred within it, in whatever style, that they work it in a way that is totally engrossing, in a way that if there were two there it would not be the same… I don't know if we talked about it but a couple of years ago I saw Ken Campbell and he was an absolute virtuoso within that particular style. He was absolutely in the middle of this thing, even though he seemed to be lurching in and out. If, on the other hand, it is simply a demonstration of virtuosity, which is not within any other context other than the personal sphere of that one artist, then I find that uninteresting. It is also uninteresting when it attains a level of narcissism, which does not admit anybody. It is a kind of demonstration of the performer in the world.

MD: What do you see as the role of your self in your solo work?

MP: In 1980 I went to Japan, to Tokyo, to study Noh and I was fortunate to study with Kanze Hideo, who is the head of the Kanze family, one of the five [main Noh theatre] families.[18] Of course whilst there are a lot of people around on a Noh stage, it is actually a monodrama. The chief performer, the shite, is the only person you are supposed to be paying attention to at all. He is the supreme performer; everyone else provides the context for him to do his thing – the musicians, the chorus. The chorus often speak his words, so he doesn't have to. His *presence* is what is extraordinary. But what is also extraordinary is that the main performers perform into old age, even though they may be performing young women. They wear a mask and you can see triple chins underneath, even a beard very clearly… and with quaking voices. But nevertheless, or even *because* of this combination, of this beautiful young mask and this aged performer, this can create deep, deep poignancy about the human condition. He is not mimicking or impersonating a young woman. There is something deeply affecting about that. So if I am talking about myself then, if I have one ambition, it is to keep doing it. You know, we never thought we would be doing this thing when we were sixty. What then might be the effect or affect for an audience, seeing me aged sixty, still doing it? Not pretending that I am twenty-three. At the CPR summer school (2008) I will be doing a RAT Theatre workshop. I am fairly convinced that most of the stuff I can't actually do, so one of my younger female colleagues will hopefully be able to demonstrate some of it. How might I appear or not appear doing any of that work? Is it interesting to see me trying to lift somebody off the ground? I don't know where that is going really. And whether I can only present all of that past work in quotation marks, so when I am doing it, I am only doing it ironically.

MD: You are kind of quoting yourself, or a younger version of yourself.

MP: That is it, precisely — very well said. Because there might be quite a lot of foolishness in seeing me attempt those things, looking like an aged Lothario. At the same time, I am getting a bit itchy, I have to say. I just

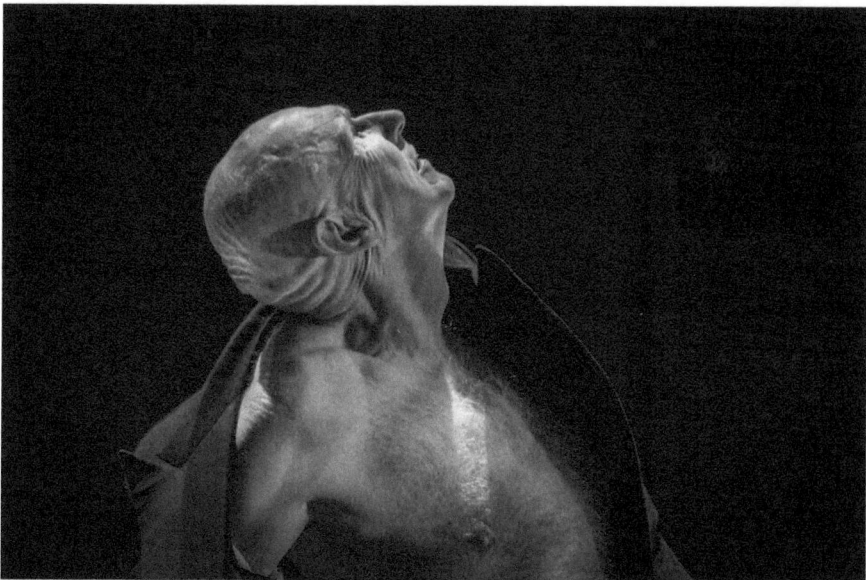

Lecon D'Anatomie, Flesh, 2014 (first performed in 1974) ©Russell Basford

feel everything is so calmed down. In our department,[19] we have a lot of audience and reception studies people and it's as if there is some kind of circuit, of audience and work referring to each other. I am waiting for the revenge of the avant-gardes really. I have to believe that some kids will say, 'Enough – let's do it this way'.

MD: Can you describe your favourite moment from a solo piece to me?

MP: If I have to think of a moment of solo performance that really profoundly influenced me, it wouldn't be a theatre one, it would be [a] music one. It was a moment upstairs here [Chapter Arts Centre, Cardiff] and it was Lol Coxhill. He was a saxophonist who played the soprano sax – very old British school.[20] He was a member of Welfare State Band[21] – their musical director for a while. He does play with other people but he has a long tradition of solo performance and he came to do a concert upstairs. He just set off. He does allude to New Orleans playing and he is very often stylistically mixed and a bit jokey. There is no policing of genre in what he does. It was a really nice time. And for some reason there had been a Socialist Workers' Party meeting during which they had all got very drunk. Somehow, they had all got in via the side door. So they were standing next to him. He is playing this really detailed free improvisation and they start shouting at him, 'Play some real music, play some real music.' He starts playing *Stranger on the Shore*, [by] Acker Bilk, on and on without stopping. And they obviously can't cope with that and they start shouting, 'Play *The Internationale*, Play *The Internationale*' and he starts playing *The Internationale*, note perfect, but on and on and on until they just leave. Then he stops and says, 'Is anybody else listening to this crap?' Then he starts to play the most beautiful version of John Coltrane's *Naima* – the most ravishing thing. I almost remember the whole experience – note for note. How he was so at the centre of his own work as a solo performer, that none of this was going to disturb him in any way. He could actually do all the trappings of what anybody ever wanted but would finally make the choice of what he thought was appropriate. It was the most startling demonstration of complete command of who he was. It wasn't about technique, but about who he was and his place in the world. Fantastic.

MD: And an ability to respond to the moment, name it and defeat it by playing. As you said, there is something about that 'on and on and on' – through repetition, giving people what they want, but to an excess. They have got to go – he gives them no option. He is not fighting.

MP: Yes exactly, exactly. That is a very strong memory of solo performance.

MD: And would you have any moments from theatre?

MP: Well, I was thinking about Min Tanaka – I will think about theatre ones in a moment – but Min Tanaka.[22] He is a very startling looking man – he is quite big so he doesn't have that diminutive [stature] of Katsuo Ohno. I saw him in Barcelona, at a large conference. There were thousands of people and all the big names in world theatre were there. I went to a lecture by Robert Wilson – incredible stuff. There was an interview session with Min Tanaka and obviously the audience knew him. And there was a question session and somebody in the audience said, 'So, Mr Tanaka, when are we finally going to see you perform in Spain?' He said, 'Now', and then he did this fantastic dance on the table. He just went 'Now'. That was amazing. That again was one of those crucial moments.

MD: Was it the moment of doing it?

MP: Yes. Again, it was that he was again so in command of his own technique, his own awareness of who he is and he could do it for a quarter of an hour of improvisation, as he would in the [stage] work. There was no need for any other context. I remember this guy in the early 1970s group called Mum's Underground. He did this whole show waiting for the group who were late. The show was about anticipating what would happen when they arrived, but of course they never did. That was very clever. And I think those are all more dramaturgical strategies about how you fill in this period of time in being a solo performer.

The greatest solo moment [in theatre] was Norman Wisdom.[23] I went to see him on my fortieth birthday. [My wife] Heike [Roms] bought it as a treat. We went to St David's Hall [in Cardiff] and the first half of the show was appalling – it was a show band with can-can dancers… Anyway, we went out for the interval, came back again and the bandleader just went up to the microphone and said, 'Ladies and Gentlemen, Norman Wisdom'. And the spotlight goes to the side of the stage and there he is – in *the* suit. And he then did his whole act – straight. I have never seen anything like it. You just thought, 'How am I watching a man who is the same age as my mother doing this'. At one point, he is strapped into a machine with boxing gloves punching him – just incredible, just incredible. People are rushing down to the front of the stage to try and touch him. The whole act – he pulled out everything, there was nothing saved. By the end, he was completely exhausted and people were cheering him on and he does an encore and he does another encore and then he comes up to the microphone, finally, after two encores, and he says 'I have only got one thing left to say – Mr Grimsdale, Mr Grimsdale' [his famous catchphase]. It was the first time he said it and I shot up in my seat and the audience went absolutely bananas. This man uses his catchphrase for the *third* encore. I mean this man really knows what he is doing. Tremendous. What was really fantastic was that at his age he knew everybody had come to see Norman Wisdom and not some replica of Norman Wisdom.

MD: There is a real thread in what you are saying about endurance.

MP: Yeah, I am interested in male performance and maybe I haven't mentioned enough female performance. But I am interested in male performance, and getting old, and endurance.

MD: You associate endurance with men?

MP: No, I don't think I do, it's just the male performances I mentioned have had a certain amount of endurance in them.

MD: I am just musing a bit on this that when you talked about your strategies for survival, you set yourself a challenge.

MP: Perhaps it's because I don't have that technique. I was thinking about Ken Campbell, who used to have a group called The Ken Campbell Road Show. It was just endless stunts, hammering nails into their noses. People like Sylvester McCoy and Dinah Stabb, they were all in the Road Show. In recent years, he does solo storytelling; it's him as a solo raconteur. We went to see him in St Donats.[24] He set off and he starts telling this story. Then he gets side-tracked. And he just goes on and on and on. Then ninety minutes later you realise that it has all come back to this story that he started off with. How it got there, I don't know. I mean, splendid. I am sure it was very, very closely scripted. But it didn't seem like it at all. All of those kinds of traditions are interesting, those comedians who can do that.

MD: There is that whole tradition in solo work of course.

MP: On the other hand, it is interesting what you were saying just now. The music hall tradition, where basically you worked on a ten-minute act. People like Little Tich, who was a very small man in very big boots. That was it. He could do point-work in boots. Fantastic.[25] As long as you don't go round [the touring circuit] too often, you could do that for the rest of your life.

MD: What do you find particular about solo working?

MP: It's the situation where you can feel most in control of the composition, I don't mean in a dominating way. If you get it right you can feel that every element has been made in the way you would most like it to be made. There is no leakage. I don't mean perfection, but you take responsibility for the whole thing and therefore I wonder if it's the thing about detail. Maybe you can work at a level of detail that is rather difficult to bring about in larger situations, with a larger group of people. When you are directing others you only ever get an approximation night after night. It's not about 'Oh I can get it right so the audience will be extra attentive and extra appreciative'. I think it is a thing about the artist... Having said that, we, in Aberystwyth, do a lot of work with undergraduates on the use of biography and autobiography and I think that there is a very counter-productive narcissistic streak now, I have to say.[26] As if telling your life story is of any interest to another group of people. One has to be aware of becoming a kind of barroom bore – the person who keeps on and on about this or that.

Increasingly, [working solo is] a kind of refresher. The amount of attention that you can give is limitless. So it is the mode within which you have to stand by your art, it is the kind of *sine qua non* – without which nothing really, Even though I forget about it for years, it is still the thing I come back to, the thing that I test myself with. I never really thought of myself as a solo artist, but it is recurrent. It always has that double edge about it. It is always an incredible challenge to keep yourself interesting for whatever period of time you have decided to do. But also the rewards that come from that are always very high, because if you do it and it succeeds then the realisation that 'I did that' are enormous. Whereas of course you are always pleased when the group succeeds but that is a communal pleasure. That solo one, that's all that performers really need.

Endnotes

1. It is therefore why I did not include the very interesting work he spoke about making with Brotzmann or with Mike Brookes from 1997, although I do include some later work to which Brookes contributes specific expertise.
2. This work is detailed in Pearson, M. & Shanks, M. (2001) *Theatre/ Archaeology*. London: Routledge.
3. This solo forms the basis of Pearson's subsequent book published in 2006, *In Comes I: Performance, Memory and Landscape*. Exeter: University of Exeter Press. Heddon writes about her re-staging of this work in Heddon, D. (2002) 'Performing the Archive: Following in the Footsteps'. *Performance Research*, 7(4), 64–77.
4. Pearson's exploratory discussion of audio walks here needs to be contextualised in that in 2007, when this interview took place, sited work and audio walks, although frequent in experimental performance, were just in the process of transitioning into more mainstream performance and visitor attraction venues.
5. Hardy is a composer, and former member of Cardiff Laboratory Theatre and Brith Gof. He was musical director on Brith Gof's large-scale works *Goddodin* (1988), *Pax* (1990) and *Haearn* (1992).
6. Sherman Cymru in Cardiff, Wales, now produces and showcases new Welsh work and also receives touring productions from other Welsh companies.
7. Woolworths was a chain store, originally founded in Pennsylvania but first opened in Britain in 1909, selling clothing, toys, sweets and music.
8. The Sheldonian Theatre is in Oxford, England, and was an early design by Christopher Wren built in 1664 for Oxford University. It houses music events, lectures, and University ceremonies and has only recently started to be used for drama.
9. *Gododdin* (1988), *Pax* (1989) and *Haearn* (1992) were all large scale, site-specific works, performed by Brith Gof in collaboration with Test Department (*Goddodin*) and Cyrff Ystwyth and Jigsaw dance company (*Pax*).

10. *From Memory* later became the title for a trilogy of solo pieces, with this section then referred to as *A death in the family*.
11. In 1985, Brith Gof had performed John Berger's *Boris*, in the barn at the Welsh Folk Museum.
12. *The Body of Evidence* (1995), which later became *Blood* (sometimes *Autopsy*) (1998).
13. Pearson goes on to describe three solo performed works he made with collaborator Mike Brookes: *Dead Men's Shoes, The first five miles* and *The man who ate his boots*. The way he spoke of them indicated to me that these were co-devised, the result of their collaborative input; Pearson in physical and textual working, Brookes in design and technological input but both involved in the overall vision of the piece. They seem to be more co-devised works therefore, and so I have not included them in this book.
14. Peter Brötzmann is a German saxophonist and free jazz improviser with whom Pearson collaborates regularly.
15. At the time, Richard Gough was a director of Cardiff Theatre Laboratory, alongside Pearson. He is now Professor in Music and Performance at the University of South Wales and artistic director of the Centre for Performance Research.
16. Forced Entertainment is a theatre company made up of six artists, based in Sheffield, England and has specialised in devising new performance since 1974. The Live Art Development agency was set up in 1999 and produces live art projects, events, publications and research in the UK and abroad.
17. Mike Brookes is a long-term collaborator and co-deviser with Pearson. They started to work together in 1997 and continue to the present.
18. Kanze Hideo was a leading 'shite' actor in Noh theatre and also professor of Art and Design at the University of Kyoto. He died in June 2007.
19. Department of Theatre, Film and Television Studies, Aberystwyth University.
20. Lol Coxhill (1932–2012), also known as George Lowen Coxhill, was an English saxophonist who was renowned for his work in the European jazz and improvised music scene.
21. The theatre company Welfare State International was founded in 1986 by John Cox, Sue Gill, Roger Coleman and others, run as a collective of artists including theatre makers, musicians and designers and originally known for their creation of large-scale outdoor events, often working with large communities of people. Their physical archive lives at Bristol University.
22. Min Tanaka is a Japanese actor and pioneer in dance, born in 1945 and a leading exponent of the radical Japanese dance–theatre form, Butoh, created by Katsuo Ohno and Tatsimi Hijikata.

23. Sir Norman Wisdom (1915–2010) was a hugely loved and esteemed slap-stick clown, comedian and actor in theatre and television, having worked in a series of famous films from 1953 to 1966, on Broadway in the USA and in television plays. He was knighted in 2000.
24. St Donats Arts Centre is at United World Colleges Atlantic College near Llantwit Major, Wales.
25. Music hall entertainer Harry Relch (1867–1928).
26. Pearson is now Emeritus Professor of Performance Studies at Aberystwyth University. At the time of interview, he was still teaching there.

Wendy Houstoun

Pact with Pointlessness (2014) ©Hugo Glendinning

Wendy Houstoun trained at the London School for Theatre and Dance (now closed) and was a founder member of the physical theatre company, DV8. It is therefore not surprising that she brings a strong focus on the body and movement to the way she thinks about and devises her work. However, while her discussion of embodied thinking in relation to areas such as her performer presence and creative making might be expected, the way she applies an acute physical intelligence to a much wider arena is perhaps not so familiar. Somatic memory, not video, is her documentation tool of choice; writing happens, for her, 'on the floor', not in a chair. She has accumulated a wealth of experience and expertise, nationally and internationally, both as a solo performer and as a member of numerous companies. She has worked across small-, medium- and large-scale physical theatre and dance work, site-specific performance, film, installation

and writing and textual work. Houstoun increasingly works intermedi-
ally, combining extended sequences of physical movement, spoken text,
interactive lighting, music and an increasing use of technology.

In these interviews, we mainly discussed five of her earlier solo works:
Haunted, Daunted and Flaunted (1995, hereafter *Haunted*), *Happy Hour*
(2001), *48 Almost Love Lyrics* (2004), *Desert Island Dances* (2007) and
50 Acts (2009). What stands out in Houstoun's conversation about
her making is how she offers an evocation of a physical sensibility and
creativity unattached to practices of display, strength, power, endurance, physical heroics or dramatic hysteria.[1] Instead, she offers a choreography, which is 'everydayish', suggestive and ambiguous. She works
continually to be present in performance, yet also speaks of her performing self as unfixable and blurry in photographs and her movement as
non-linear. One of the most enjoyable moments for me in this interview is when I ask her about 'costume' (deliberately using the language
of drama) and she laughingly admits to feeling like she is 'invisible', has
no body or definable outline. This is not however about non-existence
but about existence beyond the boundaries of human skin or gender –
the performer as moving energy. I found this a refreshing and important
non-gendered, non-macho and non-punitive evocation of a performer's
physical approach to making solo work. What also stood out for me was
her synaesthetic (i.e. brings together sensory modes) approach to making –
for example, she spoke of aiming 'to feel the shape of' the work. She
models a genuine multi-sensory approach – emphasising the importance
of light and sound (and the people who operate and design them) as
'equal partners' in her performance work and working.

In contrast to our current obsession with autobiographical confession (the memoire as extended selfie), Houstoun balks at using overt,
content-based self-narrative in her work. She details specific strategies for
precisely avoiding this kind of reading, like 'third personing', or incorporating other recorded voices into the narrative: a kind of multi-vocal
montage. However, she does suggest that her signature can be read in her
work, but more in terms of its tone and mood – often angry and provocative. This more formal approach is demonstrated vividly in her example
of translating an intense life moment, the death of her mother, into a
'hold and release, hold and release' physical hand gesture. This becomes

an 'implacable rhythm', which informs the whole of *Desert Island Dances*. The focus here is on making sense of a physical gesture rather than exposing her emotional state. This potentially leaves room for an audience to inhabit the space opened up, with their own feelings about deaths in their own families. This sense of opening up spaces, as opposed to filling them, comes across strongly in this interview.

Houstoun is eloquent about some of the challenges which are specific to solo working: as a maker–performer needing to be both inside and outside the work; having to multitask at all times and needing to not harass the material produced (knowing when to stop). She is also clear on some of the benefits of solo working: doing precisely what you want, never being late for rehearsal and not having to compromise.

Houstoun offers one very useful and perhaps unexpected model of the solo artist as always systemically connected to others, visible or not. Contrary to common assumptions of solo work as private, confessional or self-absorbed, she repeatedly describes her work as an on-going dialogue with her audience and a continual conversation with the world. This is 'personal manifesto' (15) repeatedly performed, in which she as an artist foregrounds the many social and political issues and assumptions that to her mind need questioning in our twentieth-first-century society. At one point she quotes Martin Amis: 'it's an author's responsibility to speak about being alive now'. Her performance authorship clearly fulfils this call.

Performance Chronology

After leaving college, Houstoun made work with Ludus Dance Company in London. She was involved in creating the work as well as performing in it. She was then employed by both theatre company Lumiere and Son for two years and Lloyd Newson, forming DV8 physical theatre company and performing in several of their productions for stage and film. She also started making intermittent solo work – 'to cement what had just happened with a company'. This included the smaller works she mentions here, like *Stranger in Paradise* (1986) and *My Body, Your Body* (1986), to work like *Haunted*, which was commissioned by Chisenhale Dance Space and which grew into the extended trilogy *Haunted, Daunted and Flaunted*

(1995), a monologue in eight sections. In 1996, she performed in the film 'Diary of a Dancer', directed by David Hilton, which examines the life and experiences of a fictional London-based dancer. *Happy Hour* (2001), commissioned by Chisenhale, was a site-specific piece made for bars, combining movement with extended monologue, on which she collaborated with Tim Etchells. Other site-specific solo commissions included *Reverse Effects*, produced by BITE and made for Cultural Industry in 2004, which was not discussed in this interview.[2] Then followed the studio work, *48 Almost Love Lyrics* (2004), a series of physical, recorded and spoken monologues, and *Desert Island Dances* (2007), which further combined text, movement and objects as Houstoun explored notions of utopia and paradise, absence and presence. It was co-commissioned by Southbank Centre and Danceworks UK and co-produced by Sheffield Theatres Trust. *Manifesto* (2008–2009) was a short piece which started life as a Peachy Coochy performance,[3] involving actions performed around 'yes' and 'no' statements. Some of this material was later included in *50 Acts*. *Keep Dancing*, commissioned by Dance Umbrella in 2009, also started life as a Peachy Coochy performance called *Alphabet Apology* and was first performed at the National Review of Live Arts in Nottingham and then toured internationally. At the time of our second interview, in March 2011, Houstoun had just finished making *50 Acts*, commissioned by Dance4, Nottingham, which she premiered in that month at the Nottingham Dance Festival. She went on to receive the 2013 TMA Achievement in Dance Award for this piece. *Pact With Pointlessness* is the last solo Houstoun has made to date, which she describes on her website as asking 'Big Questions' about life and death, ageing, stupidity and futility and which was created as a tribute to Nigel Charnock, who died in 2014. It premiered at the Purcell rooms in London on 5 and 6 June, 2014, and is still touring. Alongside solo work, Houstoun also makes work for other solo artists, like Antonia Grove (*SmallTalk*), as well as devising and performing regularly with companies like CandoCo Dance and Forced Entertainment.

See artists' work on

Happy Hour: https://vimeo.com/170931109; https://www.wendyhoustoun.net
50 Acts: https://www.youtube.com/watch?v=Q_OlSKnhhXc

always a helpful way. So I reacted to the difficulties I found in *Strange Fish* by using solutions like speech and third personing and lying and a kind of formalism that I hadn't used up to then – almost like a balancing act.

Happy Hour (2001) ©Chris Nashe

And then *Happy Hour* [2001] – that was a Chisenhale commission and I built that up in not a dissimilar way. Often with all of those pieces, it's about making movement from specific things I had in my mind at the time, and then working on text very separately, and then them all coming together in quite a collisional sort of way rather than moving towards a sort of logic, or structure. I tend to make pieces in short chunks, but then it's quite hard to see what they are driving at. Working with Tim [Etchells] on *Happy Hour* was very much about finding a logical form for it. Initially when I made it, I had the 'toast' things earlier and he was saying 'actually the whole thing is kind of struggling towards articulacy, so if you have the articulacy in the middle then you have made all the stuff after it redundant'. But equally a lot of the movement came from spelling. The dance behind the bar is just me spelling out, 'My name is Wendy. I am a drunk, please help me'. Or again quite formalistic things – maybe [influenced by] talking to Jonathon Burrows and people like that. I have a complete love of that very abstract and pure land, even though it is not the world I am in. We [Burrows and Houstoun] are always batting ideas between the two of us, in being foreign to each other's world, in some ways. There were also days when I would come in and just want to move, and make movement because I like doing it, and it has got no other function.

One sequence, I just did a lot, all the stuff on the floor, and then Tim had written the speech, which I learnt very separately. Doing each thing in isolation and getting very comfortable with them. And then one day, Tim was around, and throwing them both together, and they completely fitted. It was quite uncanny, how they it felt like the punctuation of one was made for the fitted speech of the other, and it was one of those very quick things that happened. I suppose that's the thing you can do because you don't have to explain to anyone why the material is there – it's just doing stuff until it finds its place. That is one of the nicest things about solo. In a way, I think it is a bit of a discipline – almost not being interested in what it is for and just allowing it to be. Clocking off and not harassing the material. Something I very much remember doing in *Haunted* was: go into the studio and do the work until six o clock. Maybe have one half an hour thinking about it, but then definitely don't harass it anymore, until you go in and do it again. So that you are not fooling yourself you are doing more work than you are, in a way. You can think that just by sitting down and thinking you are doing work and sometimes you are not. So I guess each thing comes from a mixture of some physical concern and then also some content concern. Something that maybe just keeps replaying itself.

Weirdly, the piece I recently made [*50 Acts*] has been reminding me of *Haunted* in fact. I call each section an Act. It uses video, and I ended up using a sound trigger, like a gunshot, something quite percussive that launched the next act. It's sort of a cool and hot game in a way. A lot of the transitions in this new piece are exactly the same [as *Haunted*]. Like, I rolled into that – I did exactly that. I think it is because of the act structure. I called it 50 acts and then I have to bloody well do 50 acts. My own fault. But then what became clear from almost the first three acts was they had set the rule for how things then had to go together.

MD: In your new piece or in *Haunted?*

WH: In both actually. They are quite filmic. I think they are both moving from a large expanse to a locked-down place and an opening up again. Another reason that *50 Acts* reminded me of *Haunted* is that it is just positing things all the time. It might move from a sudden drop and a roll into a mock Shakespearean speech. It uses video and manifesto and is playing the same games: changing its privacy a bit, or its intimacies.

MD: It constantly asks that question – whose fiction? There is always such a strong desire in the audience to hear a linked up autobiographical story.

WH: Yeah, and weirdly the less things are joined, as in *50 Acts* (they are really un-joined as ideas) then the audience starts making the joins instead. The surprise element. And again I think it is a bit about being on your own, where it's a way to keep your own energy changing and the nature of surprise going, conceptually. The pace can get very similar if it is only you, hammering away at the same thing.

It's weird though, because on the back of that is a conversation I have long had with Tim about making something that sticks at one project for the entirety, rather than jumping lots of projects. And actually it came up in the doing of my piece *Keep Dancing*, which we did up in Sheffield. And it was a slightly odd night and Tim came in to have a chat. I was really wanting to make a piece that had one idea and stuck at it, instead of dipping and diving around. But even within the one project, I still was dipping and diving in a cause-and-effect manner. I think it is in the nature of being on your own, but I think I prefer it: It is more refreshing for your energy to keep the game changing its mode. But Tim was saying you lose your investment in the first thing, if it keeps on altering too much.

MD: As an audience?

WH: Yes, as an audience. I mean actually in *Haunted* the project stays the same, in a way. The legal language and a sense of the re-enactment at least feels like a whole project. The way that that progresses alters but I think it probably doesn't centre the performer on a cause and effect. The next section doesn't come because the last section has been pushed to such a point where it has to change. I think dance and choreography is more used to changing its mode, from an authorial mode to a more musical one. The authorial mode is much more performer centred: you want to see them struggling with something, and then they have struggled with something, and then that is why it changes. That is a very different kind of transition... I think transitions are what I do best. I change energy, from one shape or intensity to another, and those transitions produce emotion. Changes bring emotion.

MD: How do you do that?

WH: Like when you do yoga, instead of diffusing your energy and letting it go out, you pull it in and direct it. It's like when people get a bit serious. That feels to me like they are going into a line, a bit.

MD: If one thinks in more conventional terms of how people make transitions, they will often use character or story or a cause-and-effect sequence, whereas you are saying you use energetic transitions.

WH: Or tactical ones. The thing that Tim was talking about was seeing someone try different tactics – manifold ways you can see people doing battle with an idea. That is a different game. [It's the drive for] resolutions. You don't ask that of music, actually. Like with *50 Acts*, using Chopin's preludes, which I did in Brighton. Prelude No 1 is like this. You don't [then] question why Chopin's No 2 is like it is. You don't say: 'Oh he got frustrated with No. 1 and then made No 2'. It is not of interest to me. You can say: 'Oh that one is like a funeral march, and that one is light and breezy'. The contrasts in them are what seem inevitable. It's something to do with a way of thinking about a series of studies, or musical preludes – a shift in the energies which make them right.

MD: What you are talking about here are your devising and composition methods. Have you always worked in this way?

WH: What do you mean?

MD: Making physical material and then finding texts and finding ways for them to work together. And working with compositional change using energetic shifts.

WH: Yeah probably. Yeah, and then just keep doing it every day, really. That is the other one. Just keep persisting with it. I tend not to work with video, so it's as much as remains in my memory and using what surfaces. Maybe it would be quite interesting to work with video. I have done [so] at times. Then I can't be bothered to look at it. And what do you do once you have looked at it? I mean, I am not going to recreate it.

MD: So, in terms of you documenting what you are doing, do you write things down or do you really just rely on your physical memory?

WH: If I look back over notebooks that I was using at the time, I can pretty much notice what was happening, just stuff I jot down. It's not usually very coherent and usually in the middle of everything else that is going on, so it's not a devoted notebook for that show. Next to a dentist appointment and how much money I owe and all that stuff.

MD: How do you continue to develop the work?

WH: I do have a strong eye on time. That is quite proportional to what you are making, often. That length of that requires some shift. If something has got one tone for some time, it is probably going to need to shift tone, soon. And mode as well. Working with John Avery,[7] he is quite instrumental in creating the sound, tone and also the length. I think sometimes the length of things are a bit of a problem. I often make sections in three- and eight-minute bursts. I tend to not let one idea run for much longer, so it doesn't actually mine as much as it could. I think that is quite hard to do on your own, actually.

MD: Getting away from your patterns?

WH: Just really mining the stuff from different angles. That is the problem of having to make executive decisions from outside, as well as being inside the work. You only get that mining when you are completely inside stuff, when you are with a company and you can flounder about. You are in a particular state, and you can let something much more baseline happen. On your own, it seems to me harder to relinquish the reins, because even if you are being baseline, you still need to keep your eye on people. There is no one else doing it. There is no one else there.

MD: Keep your eye on people – you mean the audience?

WH: Yeah. You can't just surrender the whole thing. Well you could, but it's very hard to come back from that, on your own. It's performatively very hard. So you tend to be always in control in one way or another, even if you are pretending not to be in control. I think that is the area that is hard and possibly impossible to deliver [in solo] – a territory of material you can mine. Which is why I think my work tends to be a certain length and stay on a particular tone.

MD: Who else do you collaborate with? You have talked so far about collaborating with Tim Etchells in terms of writing and composition and John Avery in terms of music and timing.

WH: Yes and tone, John very much sets the tone. In *50 Acts*, I [also] worked with Nigel Edwards, on lighting, towards the last couple of weeks. Partly because he has also worked with Forced Entertainment and there is an ease with [our shared] language. Nigel had quite a lot to say to me, and it is pretty vital in solo stuff that you have someone come in who you can understand their language. Because everyone has their different opinion, and when you have parades of people coming through, everyone is going to pull it towards the piece they would make. You sort of listen and sort of don't listen. One of the points of doing it [solo] is that I do what I fancy doing. But what I like about Tim and Lloyd [Newson] is that they are quite ruthless – spare, very few words, but in a quick sentence can go right to the heart of what they think the problem is. I can read what that is, and not always immediately come up with a solution, but eventually understand what that is about. Lloyd prefers things to be overtly clear in a particular way that I am not bothered about. But at the same time I can take his comments and apply them to another kind of territory. I know what he would do to the piece if he was to be in charge, but at the same time I respect what he says because I think that has some lesson for it [the piece] and some place. So those sparing but well-placed observations: they are kind of criticisms, but they are really observations.

It is quite hard to get beyond the 'that's great' as a comment. You often hear more from what people don't say, than what they do.

MD: This is collaboration as people giving you feedback, like an outside eye.

WH: With Jonathon and conversations with him, one sentence can be the thing that is backgrounding a lot of activity. Even though you are not doing anything overt about it, it still backgrounds it.

MD: Do you invite people in, or are these casual conversations?

WH: It is pretty work like. They are different to [being] social. Frank Boch is another person who comes in and is very good at being able to articulate what he sees, which is a very hard thing to do. To a degree it almost doesn't matter whether I am going to accept it or not. The act of even starting to do something in a room is always the most embarrassing bit, really. In the daylight, saying 'I am going to come on from here and they are sitting there' and then you actually have to do it. It is just humiliating, really, for everyone concerned (laughs).

MD: I know – that moment of starting.

WH: I just laugh. You feel so stupid. 'I just made it up'. Especially if it is the first time you have shown somebody anything. You think you have gone mad. I suppose that was the bonus with *Happy Hour*, where Tim saw the piece at certain points and then worked on it from there. And that was a useful method; because I think on your own, it is pretty useless to start from scratch with someone. Unless they are going to be there all the time, then it's redundant in terms of contact. So I think it is better to have something, and then if that is the thing that connects with someone, then that makes sense. 'Yes, I spotted something in that which interests me', so that makes sense of why they are going to be there, carrying on with it. Rather than – 'ok we have got to make a piece together'. I don't always understand that as a thing.

MD: I was speaking to Nigel [Charnock] yesterday and he was saying he is a purist… solo is solo and for him no one comes to see him.

WH: He would, wouldn't he? Yes, absolutely, that is his thing.

MD: From watching an early fragment of *Haunted*, it is really clear that lighting and sound is critical and woven into the work. Can you tell me more about how you worked on the sound with John?

WH: John Avery is fundamental. *Haunted* was the first project we worked on. He would generally come in and there would be very little to see, as far as I was concerned. I would just be pottering about. He would come and sit. I would resist it actually. I didn't really like anyone watching until I thought I had something. But actually I think it was more useful for him to see what I was working with. He would offer sound stuff in quite early, actually. And Steve Munn as well.[8] Steve lit the [full] show. He used to be at the Laban centre. He used to get four or five days' production time there, as part of the making process. The first fifteen minutes – it might have been on the back of them, and extending it, that Steve lit the whole piece. He was designing it. It was planned. My memory is of him watching it, putting the lights up and then the transitions are the things that almost come because another element is added actually. Because I think most of the tracks would have been of indeterminate lengths. And the decisions for those then crystallise where the real transition is, really. That is why I like technical things. The transitions were made through practical decisions, and they are rhythmic. And then [we would] show it to the students. It was so sculptural. I am sure a lot of things came with the light.

MD: With the lighting operation, did you rehearse it?

WH: Yes and actually a design can be dramatically altered by whoever is operating it. By a sensitivity or an insensitivity. Now, not being able to afford someone, you only get someone who has seen the show that day and you get approximations. You don't really get this lived-in feel. It's in the whole nature of how popular the piece is, because if you get a lot of bookings, you can really work the performance a bit. By 1997 *Haunted* had had a lot of performances in a lot of places. So it is quite worked as a performance. Now, I am lucky if I do a performance ten times, spread over two years. So the chances of that ever looking sharp and succinct, or worked rhythmically [are rare]. That is the same for a lot of work, which is why a lot of work looks neither here nor there. Because it never gets a run. Never gets lived in. Except for the really big stuff. And then that looks overworked. Pop versions…

Haunted (1995) ©Chris Nashe

The work itself is part of an on-going discussion I am having. In a way I see all working like that. It's continuous dialogue, about why you are doing it, and what's important to do. When I was touring earlier this year, I was reading a David Mamet thing about the purpose of a lot of work being to balance the inside and the outside. Atmospherically, or politically, a situation can change, and what is required to balance that out can be different at any given moment. It goes all sorts of ways, but to me there is some on-going dialogue, and trying to notice what is happening, seeing as you are alive. I really like writers. I read an awful lot and I like to hear what they have to say about the act of writing. I remember reading Martin Amis: 'it's an author's responsibility to speak about being alive *now*'. It feels like an on-going negotiation, trying to understand what is happening, your response to it and any other response that may be needed at any given point.

MD: Yes, especially as there are also often silences around things or situations are just accepted, normalised – and your job is to highlight them.

WH: Like with *48 Love Lyrics*, I remember reading Deborah Hay[9] quite a lot; about ways she framed questions around the body. In a way I felt like that piece was more about its tone than its content. *How* it was done was more important than *what* it was – *how* I was on stage more vital than any other material. Just being very present and keeping my hands off of every other thing. Just that activity.

MD: I remember the tone of *48 Almost Love Lyrics* as being full of anger.

WH: Maybe a George Bush moment.

MD: What does the term 'solo' conjure up for you?

WH: I tend to think of it [solo] as an activity that [paradoxically] helps you work with other people. It means you are able to offer in and keep functioning as a making person within a group. With Forced Entertainment (FE) and DV8 and pretty much anybody I was working with, they wouldn't be working with you as someone who is told what to do. I think the flexing of the muscles and making choices and devising and just knowing how bloody hard it is actually makes you very much more considerate and allows room in a company. If you understand that, you are going to be offering in a very different way to someone who doesn't. In a way, solo stuff isn't a crusade for me. It's very much part of an ongoing dialogue, but also a way of being. So when you do work with other people, you have got routes in, ways of offering stuff forward, which, if you don't have, you are in a hard position. If something comes up as an idea in the space, it means I have a mechanism and a way into developing it without having to wait for someone else to give me a plan. So for me it [solo] is a kind of vital thing, relevant to working with other people as well. I tend to think it is a good antidote. If it was the only thing I did, I couldn't imagine sustaining it. But it tends to go to and fro – working with a company to going back to working on my own, to working with a company. And probably for a good reason. After being with FE, even just being here in Toynbee and doing my own stuff, your doubt [about your own work] has increased, but also your confidence increases. Both sides of the coin. The muscle gets played out in a much stronger way, than with a gang, where you are particularly inside it and blissfully relinquish quite a lot of decision-making and the faff around the edges, with applications and money and organisation.

MD: Is there anything we have missed about your solo methods of working?

WH: I have a feeling that writing will become more and more important to me as a practice. But it has to always be based in some physical act. It is not something [for me] that is a sitting and thinking thing. This woman Charlotte asked me to do research with her, to go in as a writer. But I think she has got a limited idea of what a writer is: as someone who sits and watches and then goes away and writes. But actually, unless I am moving, I won't come up with any ideas for writing anyway. It is not divorced from activity to me. I need to talk to her before we start because she thinks I am going to deliver one definite thing and I don't function like that. I could try, but I have a feeling it would be very dead, if I did it like that.

MD: When I am working with Chris [Crickmay], one exercise we do to get material is one of us starts moving solo, and the other person witnesses this and then both of us write – not *about* the movement, but writing *from* the movement – associations, ideas, whatever comes up from what you have just done, moving or witnessing. Your ideas and images come from very different places when you do these kinds of actions, as opposed to a sitting thinking action.

WH: Even in *Desert Island Dances*, the description of the Fantasy Island only came about because of moving a lot and thinking about it much more pictorially and then it was condensed down into a verbal thing. I don't think my imagination functions in a purely linguistic way. I am not quite sure how it does at the moment, so I would be interested to find out.

MD: Well, moving does something to you. It changes you.

WH: Yeah. I suppose it is something about writing on the floor as opposed to writing on the page. The better things that I have done verbally have tended to be written through talking them out rather than through pen and paper. But they have also come about partly through different people's responses – again through seeing pieces. They respond quite strongly to the verbal parts of the piece, as much if not more than the movement parts.

MD: Can you say more about this relationship between moving and writing, for you?

WH: I think it is about trying to detect the place that you are most comfortable. I think it is quite hard to give yourself permission to be in the place that is the most comfortable, especially with movement, which has a tradition of self-criticism and self-laceration. When I think of the bits of text that I quite like, like the island thing in *Desert Island Dances* or the throwing-out speech in *Happy Hour*, some of those bits of talking don't even feel like they were being made coz they feel like: 'Yeah I'll just do that because it really makes sense'. There is some ease about it. It is quite hard to land on those places as well. I wonder if it's about [me] beginning to identify a place where [I have] probably more of a natural tendency [i.e speaking]. With movement, it is something I like, something that is learnt and investigated with curiosity but maybe not such a natural tendency as language. I have a sense of that as time goes on. I think you probably get distilled as you get older – distilled down to more of the essence of something. That is part of my suspicion that I am harbouring about myself. I shall wait to see if it is true (laughs).

MD: What is the role for your self in your solo work?

WH: I don't think about it too much, because it is going to be there. You are not going to avoid that one. I also don't think you can taper what people see of you, actually, but they are always going to watch the thing you don't want them to look at. I find that people always think that solos are confessional and deeply autobiographical, and probably everything is because you came up with it. I just don't set out with that as my principle, increasingly, nowadays. Maybe when you are younger you try to have your say on what goes on. But as time goes on, you realise you haven't got any say anyway and it's a bit too late… Yeah, that autobiographical thing. If it is overt, I find it ugly to watch, and so I increasingly try not to put it in. It is there at moments, but…

MD: If it is overt in other people's work?

WH: Yes. If the main drive is for someone to tell me about their life, I think 'for fucks sake'. In some ways I remember Gary [Stevens][10]... saying ages ago – I did a piece and he said, 'oh it's like a manifesto, a personal manifesto' and I think there is something in the nature of that in my work. Trying to assert what I believe in. Making a stand for stupidity and for things like that, which I think are very important. Being able to mouth off if you fancy it and look a bit ugly. I think of it [autobiographical working] more in that sense, these days, than I do as self-representation or trying to relay any particular event. I mean in my last piece, there was some stuff in there about my mum dying, but in a way that was as much about documentation. In *Desert Island Dances*, it really is just a hand movement, like this, and by repeating it, I am trying to understand, or get to grips with it.

MD: What movement was it?

WH: Lying on the ground, a sort of hand-grasp-release: something I remember her doing. [It looked like] a clinging on, emotive thing [but I am sure] it was completely physiological: release and grasp, release and grasp, physiological and arrhythmic. There was an implacable rhythm about it, that was then thematically in the piece. [In relation to autobiographical content in my work], I also talked to Terry in FE a while ago about the difference between some people who are quite linear and some people who use energy. In dance, I am very conscious of almost two separate groups of people. Some people are very good at striking line and shape, and being very clear in space. I have always felt very diffuse. I had to learn line. I tend to work off energy, more in shifts of energy.

And that is [an example of] a kind of 'self-narrative format' if I think of anything. *Haunted* 'seemed' to be directly about everything but it was, 'No, I am speaking because I want to be able to lie, I am not speaking because I am telling you exactly what happened'. It's quite interesting – there is no getting away with it if you are on your own, then people always think that it is all about that [autobiography]. I don't know how you get away from that.

MD: Well, there are different devices – third person-switching persona.

WH: 'I know you know I know'.

MD: In *Haunted*, one of the things going through my mind was – 'is that true… ?' And I got pleasure in not knowing that… in a way I don't really care. I mean I do care, as you were talking about rape – of course I care. But to me you signalled that it was not 'about' you…

WH: Yeah, that's not the point of it. I think what is more autobiographical [in the work] are the mood tones, because they are the things we use frequently. I tend to always get cross at some point. It's what I do.

MD: What about you and what you are wearing. How do you 'costume' yourself?

WH: I remember getting a review that said, 'She is dressing for comfort' so – not like 'costume'.

MD: Some people might intentionally not use their own clothes because they do not want not to be read as 'themselves' at all.

WH: Yeah. I don't know. It's never been something that interests me. There was another jacket and then there had to be a replacement jacket, not as nice as the one used before. I think I vary the tops as well. When it first started I had a weird pink crepe top. I am not sure why I wore that. There is something weird with clothing and it might sound a completely absurd thing to say but there is a bit of me that doesn't think I am visible. (MD and WH laugh) I know I am and I am making a piece, but I actually think I am making pieces that are more [about working with] energy. That I am not actually a shape. So when I see my image, I think: 'Oh God that is a bit weird. I have got an outline', because I don't feel like I have got one, if you know what I mean. That is why I also think 'clothes – oh – clothes – on what?' If I started tending to it too much, it would dramatically alter the nature of what I do. I have often thought I am someone based on energy. But I never think of being linear, or someone who makes lines. Some dancers you see are always making lines or shapes. There are relatively few photos of me in things, really because of that reason. I don't actually make a good photo, because I am slightly blurry… And people will always watch something around the edges of the thing that you think you are talking about anyway. They will always end up looking at the way you are standing and what they think that means, as

Pact with Pointlessness (2014) ©Hugo Glendinning

much as what you are saying. So there is no way to circumscribe people's perception, in a complete way. It is pointless to try.

MD: Can you describe a moment from your favourite solo?

WH: I am trying to think of solos I have seen… I don't see very much. In my own work, it's a movement: they tend to be fall-rise things… It's that thing from *Haunted* – pulling back and then rolling to the ground and then coming up. I don't know why. I tend to like falling. I'm good at falling. Because it is fluid as well – you know where you are going. Everything else is a decision, at some point. It is quite a contained little sequence, which repeats itself… Some moments have frames around them and other moments don't. I often ask people what things they can remember from dance pieces, because much movement works in a much more wallpaperish fashion. [Specific moments] are quite few and far between, I realise. They become defining movements connected with people, like Anna Teresa's … sort of (swish gesture).

MD: My question was what was your favourite *moment* in a piece, and what you are focusing on is a *movement* moment.

WH: Oh – maybe I read it as movement – I am slightly blind… (Laugh)

MD: Misreading is fine, but the question is still your favourite moment…

WH: It would still probably tend towards a physical moment because that has the clearest impression on me. I am interested when audiences go very still, [like] the other day when we did *Bloody Mess* at Queen Elizabeth Hall and the shouting bit at the end.[11] I walked around the space and I always tend to think if you notice how high spaces are, it really helps you understand. That place is enormous and at the back you are behind – it's quite a weird space, it's got two lighting grid things that are quite low down at two points through the auditorium so I finally understood why if you are in the back bit you feel very disconnected from the stage (1.01) and it's because you are behind a low bit of concrete – its deceptive – you think it is all one room but actually if you go to the back you feel like you are in another room a bit and it's really high and I took that into account and I know that when I shouted I really surprised myself how loud I shouted but I was thinking of this height and people went really still. All I remember thinking is that people had gone really quiet, what's the matter? I didn't know it was to do with something I had done – you know. It was a really weird moment – and actually whenever that can happen, those moments are really interesting. There used to be a moment in *Haunted* where I knew if I held my breath it would go really really quiet and it did. And it was something I could manipulate at a certain point, just by holding my breath and counting to five. You could just still people. There is something about that – if that ever happens it is really good. I don't think you can divorce a good moment on stage from an audience. That would be a moment.

MD: What is next for you?

WH: I still have a lot of questions about formats. Theatrical touring is starting to feel very lumpy and a heavy way to move things about. Maybe it is the length and the format and about going back to shorter stuff and not ambitioning to make an entire piece from the beginning. Or even what the nature of stuff is. I have more questions than I have anything to say, I think. I am always struck with how Tim can set up these really interesting ways to solicit material but in a way that doesn't feel like leaning on people too heavily. I think it is very hard to come up with those constructs, without feeling that you are just preying on people. There is something about those formats that expose the individual in a multiple way, that I think is really interesting and is more about solo than one person getting up and doing a solo, in a funny way and yet I can't think of a format that would do that. Multiple answers to one thing and being somebody that holds something rather than someone who is at the centre of it?

And [I have] a question with movement and dance and how you get to feel quite everydayish about it and not trying so hard. Relaxing a bit more. And then how to finance a coherent creative life – one of my biggest questions at the moment. Not bounding from one place to another. My patience is growing very thin. And it feels quite juvenile, a lot of the time, this theatre thing. It feels quite hard to just let it be itself. There is something about the claims that you have to make, versus the thing you want to do, and then what that ends up being surrounded with. That starts to affect everything, from marketing to raising the money, to where you put it on, to audience figures. It's where the practical work collides with the more ideal situation and that is something I don't seem to have really cracked in all this time and that bothers me a bit. Because time is running out. How to have some control over how you are doing things…

Endnotes

1. This is a gendered debate, where the dominance of traditional and decidedly masculine physical aesthetics (of endurance, violence, extremes) are repeatedly evoked, in the work of theatre practitioners like Artaud, performance theorists like Hans Thies Lehmann or philosophers like Theodor Adorno and Jean-Francois Lyotard. I discuss this in further detail in my doctoral thesis, *Devising Solo Performance: A Practitioner's Enquiry.*

2. Other site-specific works made by Houstoun include *Mind The Gap* (date?) for the South Bank Centre and *Take Me to the River* (date?) for the South Bank and Greenwich & Docklands Festival.

3. I was introduced to the performance format, Peachy Coochy by Houstoun in her first 2007 interview, in which artists are invited to make a performance using twenty slides, each of which is shown for twenty seconds.

4. J.M. Coetzee wrote his novel *Foe* in 1986, based on Daniel Defoe's novel, *Robinson Crusoe*. Mark Wheatley and Complicite, in a co-production with West Yorkshire Playhouse, adapted *Foe* for performance in 1996, in part explored through these devising workshops.

5. The National Theatre of Brent was started in 1980 by Patrick Barlow, initially with Julian Hough and then a variety of other actors, and is a comedy act. They performed initially as a two-man theatre troupe doing versions of large-scale events, like The Charge of the Light Brigade, or The Messiah.

6. *Strange Fish* was a dance-theatre piece conceived and devised by physical dance-theatre company DV8 in 1992, and later made into a film. Houstoun played a leading role.

7. John Avery is an English sound designer, composer and solo performer, originally part of the band Hula in the early 1980s and 1990s and since then collaborating with solo artists, theatre companies and also working alone.

8. Steve Munn is artistic director and CEO of Déda, a centre for creative dance in Derby.

9. Deborah Hay is a postmodern choreographer, dancer and writer and was one of the founding members of the collective Judson Dance Theatre in New York in 1962–1964.

10. Gary Stevens makes performance and installations and is a tutor on the BA Fine Art course at the Slade School of Fine Art, University College, London.

11. Houstoun is referring to a theatre piece she worked on and toured with Forced Entertainment, this performance being at the National Theatre in London in 2010.

Nigel Charnock

Dixon Road (2012) ©Hugo Glendinning

The late Nigel Charnock was a vibrant, physical choreographer and performer, who created dazzling, challenging performances. Over a career spanning thirty years, he worked with renowned companies such as DV8 and Helsinki City Dance Theatre Company, as well as working alone. He was well known for his high energy dance work, blended with an oratorical, prophet-like, provocation of his audiences – a highly effective and exquisite irritant. Within the whole set of interviews he provides an example of a well-defined solo practice, using an explicitly autobiographical approach, in order to weave personal concerns about existence, death, love, and relationships into a much larger tapestry of global issues concerning religious wars, territorial occupation, prejudice and racism.

The solo works we discussed included *Resurrection* (1991), *Heroine* (1995), *Hell Bent* (1994), *Human Being* (1997) and *Frank* (2001).

His work is distinctive in that he clearly felt no need to categorise himself as belonging to one particular discipline – switching between visual, physical and spoken–sung styles of performance whenever needed. He also defies categorisation as either an experimental artist or a popular one, switching freely between vocabularies according to what the work needed. His solo work therefore includes ballet and tap, release dance and pedestrian movement, combining both improvised and set choreographies. His vocal work spanned improvised monologues addressed to the audience, rehearsed poetic texts, as well as songs from jazz and musical repertoires. He always worked with music, both existing and newly created, collaborating regularly with musician and composer Nicholas Skilbeck.

Charnock as a performer was in many ways a dancing, speaking contradiction: intensely personal, yet political; insulting, yet entertaining; patronising, yet humble. In this, he deliberately exploited certain stereotyped views of the solo performer–creator, wilfully taking on the role of a prima donna – arrogant, volatile, virtuosic – and a loner, as well as other personas. This contrasts with some other practitioners in this book, who have chosen to reveal opposite qualities, namely: low key, collaborative, reflective and not concerned to 'entertain'. While Charnock insisted that solo for him meant working purely alone, he then goes on to describe a close collaboration with Skilbeck. While arguing for a purist approach to what an improvised work should be – namely, without any planning beforehand – he then describes how his improvised solo *Frank* was actually structured around a series of songs. In both his practice and speaking about this practice, he thus adopted a number of contradictory positions, without feeling the need to resolve them into a neat, uniform package.

Nevertheless, it is true that Charnock is alone amongst the practitioners interviewed in largely using just one artist's contribution to his work. When he did involve another person (as a composer), this was just to add to the content of the work, not to its wider structure or dramaturgy. He did not customarily consult anyone else as 'outside eye', director, dramaturg or choreographer. Instead, he operated as a practitioner solely in (internal) dialogue with himself, combining the multiple roles of deviser, writer, designer, director and performer.[1]

In this interview, I chose to focus much of the discussion on Nigel's popular improvised solo *Frank*, which started as a one-off performance for the Vienna Biennale, in 2001, but, due to its popularity, was subsequently performed more than 150 times. This is a rare occurrence in solo contemporary performance, where new work, if popular, most usually tours intensively early in its existence and is then superseded by other work. It is also very rare for an improvised piece to receive such long-term performance exposure. Nigel offered unique insights into what happens to an improvised work when performed repeatedly over time.

Performance Chronology

Resurrection (1991) was Charnock's first solo, a dance-theatre piece including songs and engaging in themes of love, loss, redemption and loneliness. Charnock spoke of this work as being created in reaction to making the DV8 piece, *Dead Dreams from Monochrome Men* (1988), and therefore he used spoken words as well as movement, and offered a light, humorous tone, which came to characterise his later works. His next solo, *Hell Bent* (1994), was inspired by the drawings by Francis Bacon, and again took the form of a direct address monologue to the audience, exploring explicitly the public and private aspects of Charnock's character. It again included spoken text and dance, with original songs and music by Nicholas Skilbeck. Charnock then made *Heroine* (1995), a biographical piece based on the life of Billie Holliday and, after several other group pieces, he created *Human Being* in 1997. Garbled – trying to say too much in one sentence? He speaks of this as a piece in which he aimed to condense and simplify his artistic and aesthetic concerns. His curiosity and questioning about human existence became a focused exploration of birth and death and his visual aesthetics were pared down into very simple staging and costume. This striving for simplicity culminated in his improvised solo, *Frank*, in (2001), where once again he limits the visual mis-en-scène to his moving body through space and light. He again uses dance-theatre and spoken word, in direct address to an audience whom he harangues, flatters and climbs over, grilling them about their attitudes to life, love, religion and politics. Charnock traces, in this interview, how

Frank changed from being an extended improvised dance-theatre piece in the first two years of touring, to being a vehicle for him to explore his existential thinking about dualism and its transcendence through performance. Charnock made or was involved in several other non-solo works after this interview, including *Stupid Men* (2008) and *Nothing* (2010), as well as continuing his choreographic work with the Helsinki City Dance-Theatre. He continued to be passionate, obstinate and opinionated until his death from cancer in August 2012.

Artist's works: https://www.facebook.com/nigelcharnockarchive/

The Interview

MD: Are you working on a solo at the moment?

NC: I am touring a solo, *Frank*. I have been touring it for five years.

MD: That's a long time.

NC: Yes, it's a long time. It doesn't feel like it because a lot of it is improvised. It feels different every time I do it, so it's not the same show. And even if it wasn't improvised, I am doing it in front of different audiences, countries, and different nationalities. That changes it quite a lot as well. And I don't do it every week. I haven't done that many performances; 150, I suppose.

MD: So was that a conscious decision – to make the solo and then tour it for a long time?

NC: No, in fact I didn't want to make a solo. I had made four or five before that, and I thought, 'that's enough; I don't want to do solo work anymore. It's lonely, it can be depressing.' I had found out enough about myself as a performer. Making a solo takes six weeks and I didn't want to do that again. I am getting older. I don't like rehearsing – I don't mind doing it with other people, but on my own, it's totally boring. But then, at the Venice biennale, they said 'Look we will give you this money; we are having a festival of male solos. Will you make a solo for us?' I needed the money, so I said yes, but I kind of lied, because I didn't rehearse it. What I did was find music I really liked to dance to. I spent most of the time in HMV, choosing music. I put the songs in order; I've got quite good at that over the years. How I make work with other people is that I have all these bits and then, as it comes towards the end, I start to put them in a certain order. It's a bit like making an album. You don't put four ballads together, often. You will have a ballad, and then maybe another ballad, and then you will put in an up-tempo thing. It is the same kind of thing theatrically or dance wise. I don't like to have a lot of slow music and slow dancing and then something very fast. I will have slow, or very very fast and then not so fast, and then quite slow, and then suddenly very very fast and then quite slow. I arranged the music like that. Also, I knew that I wanted the Bach at the very beginning, because it is so spiritual and uplifting. And I wanted the Mozart at the end, because it is an overture, so should not be at the beginning. It is such amazing music and really stirring and it's great to have a full orchestra. So I had a beginning and an end, and then arranged the things in the middle.

Frank (2001) ©Nick Mercer

MD: So you arranged the piece with a notion of composition and rhythm. You are talking about the rhythm, aren't you?

NC: Yes, I am. Light and shade and all the rest of it. Then I came here [The Drill Hall] for two or three days, for three hours a day, and I put this music on and danced to it. I just improvised, I didn't set anything, and that was that. I don't find it difficult to interpret music. But that has taken many years. If ten years ago you said, 'Ok, I'm going to put ten different pieces of music on and I want you to dance to them', I would have found it quite difficult. Now I would be able to do something straight off. But that is through years and years of working with music. And when I am dancing just to music, there is always a story–narrative line going on in my head. It's a huge discussion, isn't it? What happens when the brain hears music? Anyway, then I went off to Venice and I just did it. And since then, it has grown into something else.

I set it off, I initiated it, but now it's something else – it's a monster or it's a beautiful thing. It really tells me what to do now. When I am performing, I begin and then it happens, and then it seems to end, and actually during it, it's a little bit like me being absent from the whole thing. I used to think that performing was about being present, in the moment, and I think it is, but it's also at the same time about being absolutely absent, and not being there at all. Particularly in improvisation, and in solo improvisation. When you are with other people, it's different, and you have got to be there a bit.

MD: Is that something that you found working with it from the beginning?

NC: No, that has taken a few years. I think I was doing a 'show' for about two years, with *Frank*. I was improvising, and then because I had a bit of a life change (my philosophy and my thinking changed), then the show changed as well. Which is another good thing about improvisation. Whatever happens in my life, it feeds into the show. Because the show is not scripted, I don't have to think 'I'm supposed to say this and I don't want to say it anymore. I don't feel like this anymore, about life and death and sex'. With improvisation, you can just change it on the night. I will read the newspaper that afternoon, and something from the news will pop into my head on stage, and I can actually say it.

MD: When was your first performance?

NC: It was in Venice in 2002, at the end of these twenty-five male solos that had been going on for weeks. I was on the last night. So I went up there, and a weird kind of relaxation came over me. Now I get more terrified before I am performing *Frank*, but for that first show, I wasn't. I just thought, it doesn't really matter, because it will only be one night. I am not going to do this again, so who cares? I don't give a fuck, I'm just going to go up there and dance to some music I like, and say some things in between. That gave me an enormous amount of freedom. So I went out and did it, and it was a big success. Particularly in Italy – the Italians love my stuff, because it's very theatrical and passionate and all the rest of it. So we started saying, 'oh, maybe we should do this again somewhere?' Then it started; the next tour after that was in the summer of 2002 and then the spring of 2003.

MD: How did the piece develop? You mentioned a couple of years of doing it. What exactly was 'doing it'?

NC: If I can go back to the other solo work? All the other solos were strictly choreographed and written. I learnt the lines, and steps. That really is doing a show and it got really boring, and I got depressed. I don't know how people do musicals in the West End. They go in every night for five or six years. Like the last solo I did – *Human Being* – doing that show night after night and touring around, it became like a job. Also the thing about solo work is that you are on your own, obviously. But I am really, really on my own. There is no director, no video, and I don't have a mirror. Nobody comes in and sees it before we do the first night. So it is just me and a technician, touring around. I am continually going over the script and changing things. Every venue we would go to, I would have to be there in the morning to warm up, and to do the dress rehearsal in the afternoon, and the sound check. And I thought, 'please, this is like work, and I don't want to work, really'. I had a good time doing it – I toured a lot of the solo work. But I decided, when it came to *Frank*, I just didn't want to do that anymore; it just felt like a waste of time. It also occurred to me when I see theatre, or dance, even when I listen to music, or look at paintings, or read a book – it's dead. There is dead art and there is live art, and the dead art is something that is recorded – it is something that is done in the past. Even in forms of so-called live theatre, people are in front of you and repeating something that they have learnt in their heads. They are saying lines that they have learnt, and they are moving about the stage in probably exactly the same way as they did in the last performance, and probably will do the next night. In dance as well, you have people repeating something. To me, theatre is supposed to be about creativity, not about repetition. What I see a lot of the time is artists just re-presenting something in front of you, which is kind of dead. It smells of death. Even if it is the first night, I just think, 'Oh dear, I can just smell the rehearsal and studio and I can smell them counting in their heads and "getting it right".' That is another thing; there is so much 'getting it right'. Because you learnt this thing and somebody has told you what to do. And then you have to repeat that, and get it right. And I just think that that is hideous for art, or any kind of creativity. There is no wrong or right, in art. That is what I had been doing for years, and that is why I am now into improvisation. Although, now I have been doing *Frank* for such a long time, I am repeating things, particularly in the dance, because the music makes me move in a certain way. But I aim to make it alive as possible, in the moment. For me, that is what theatre is particularly about – it is that moment of liveness. Of course, some performers are brilliant, and it is their job to make it seem like it is improvised, even if they are doing the same steps for years. And some choreographers are brilliant, because they choreograph these movements on dancers that you just want to look at. I don't think I am very good at that. So I think the reason why I am into improvisation now is trying to make it a live piece, rather than a dead piece.

MD: And how did you decide on what to wear in *Frank*?

NC: I wanted to start the piece in my pyjamas. I feel quite relaxed in my pyjamas, and I didn't want this to be some great big huge performance thing where I am wearing make-up and wigs and all the rest of it. I wanted to keep it as simple as possible. And I thought, 'Ooh I just want to start in light clothes' and then I found this Smedley top, blue, which is something to do with the sky and links to the first music, the Bach, about St John's passion and death or salvation. The first movement stuff is in a spotlight, and it is me trying to get up, trying to go to heaven or the sky. I am constantly trying to go up into the light. And so I wanted to have light clothes on as well. It is about light and brightness, rather than the dark thing.

MD: But you wear your own clothes? You don't have someone else make you something?

NC: Ooh no, never – I have never worked with a costume designer; I don't see the point. Ninety-eight per cent of the time, I know what I want. If I work with a set designer, or a costume designer, they are artists and they want to create something. So it really is a collaboration with another artist and that is very difficult for me. Because to collaborate with other artists really well, you have to find somebody on the same wavelength as you. Usually I know what I want. And I will never wear clothes that I have bought before. They will always be specially bought. Also, I never wear those clothes in public, off stage.

MD: What does that separation do for you?

NC: It's a big cliché, but when I put the clothes on that I am going to perform in, then I think, 'Ah right, this is now a performance, this is different. This is not real life, this is not an ordinary thing. It is abnormal, super normal'.

MD: Can I take you back to you saying there is no wrong and right? Performing improvisation takes confidence. Is it ever wrong?

NC: No. I really don't think there is a wrong and a right.

MD: So have you not seen any improvisation that makes you think 'Oh my God, no.'

NC: Oh yeah, but I think, this is so arrogant, all the [so-called] improvisation that I have seen, which is not a lot, is not improvisation. These people are not improvising: Juleyn Hamilton, that is not improvisation. He admits that it is not improvisation, because there are all these little cues, and they have been rehearsing for two or three hours. Even people who are improvising to some kind of structure – like a piece of music or 'oh well – we will do that', or, 'your relationship to her is this and you maintain that relationship' – for me as soon as you have any kind of structure or rule, then it is not improvisation in the strictest sense of the word. That is why I say *Frank* isn't really improvised, particularly the music and dance. The spoken bits in between are, I think. This new piece that I have just done, *Stupid Men*, with four of us on stage improvising, that for me really is improvised, because there is absolutely nothing planned. There is just an empty stage. There is no discussion beforehand on anything. We just go on and we have the technical guy who rings this bell after sixty minutes and that's when we know to stop. In a way, even that is not improvised, of course, because I know that we are on stage and there are other people with me for sixty minutes. So that is already a kind of structure. But I think it's more of an improvisation than having a specific structure or certain pieces of music that you know are going to happen.

MD: Some might say that what is deathly, in improvisation, is absolute freedom.

NC: Oh, absolutely. People are terrified of absolute freedom. People go on about 'oh I want to be free, I am an artist and I want to express myself.' They are talking a load of crap. People are deeply fearful of freedom; they do not want freedom. You give people total freedom and they cannot handle it. People cry and throw themselves around – it's just awful. So you can't just give them total freedom, it doesn't work.

MD: Or improvisers can get very general – which can also get boring.

NC: Yes. That is because some people feel improvisation is about playing, or it's about being like a child again. I am constantly saying: 'This is a performance. You can't stand there and have a quiet conversation about something – what are you doing? This is not normal, natural behaviour. This is hyper-real and abnormal and obscene and lewd and disgusting and immoral'. It's not just about being a child again in a playground, or having a party. For me, it's the hardest work. It's much easier for me to repeat something I have learnt. With improvisation, it's a very subtle thing – it's like tuning in a radio somewhere in Poland. It's very delicate and fragile. Sometimes you get it… It's about being absolutely out of control, and absolutely in control at the same time. And it's also that thing about being absolutely present, and absolutely absent, at the same time.

MD: What comes up again and again in your conversation is your pleasure in making and performing. You are clearly doing what you like. How do you also guard against that turning into self-indulgence? It is the minefield that solo practitioners move through, isn't it?

NC: I think it is always remembering that this is a performance, and this is not for you as a performer, this is for the audience. It's about communication. It is that thing about putting myself in an audience's point of view and looking back at me. And also, it is about entertainment. I like to entertain people and make them laugh, and move people and communicate with them. Most of the time, I am not thinking I am making art, or something very worthy or political. I am there to entertain people, to stop them thinking about their fucking awful dreadful lives for a few minutes. I want to say something by being it – being that thing I am trying to communicate. If an audience feels that you are flying by the seat of your pants, it makes them feel 'well, if he can get up there in front of all us, and almost make it up as he goes along, then can't I do that with my life as well?'

MD: Would you now say that improvisation is your primary devising strategy?

NC: What?

MD: I talked with Sten Ruudstrom who practices Action Theatre, [created by Ruth Zaporah], which includes training in improvisation techniques. I knew that asking him about his 'devising strategies' as an improviser was contradictory in one way, but also real, as you can pin down improvisation practices, like being in the moment, fast decision-making, returning to material, shifting energy…

NC: Yeah yeah – it's difficult to ask someone who is improvising about their strategy, because if there is a strategy then it is not true improvisation really. The day before I am going to do *Frank* I go very quiet, and depressed and worried. I used to look around for things that I could use in the show that night. And then nearly always, once the show had begun, I would forget, and afterwards I would go back into the wings and say, 'oh I didn't use that' and I would have felt glad that I didn't. Any kind of planning or strategy – it negates improvisation.

MD: What about the embodied things in you that come out – somatic memory? In one way, you are talking about present time planning, but what about dealing with the 'planning' that is already inside you?

NC: Yeah. Now I do much more technical things than I have ever done. For me warming up takes a long time, and I do everything. I do every kind [of] boring exercises. I do ballet, loads of sit-ups, Pilates, yoga, all for about two hours. That is during the day and then about two hours before the show I warm up my voice. I do these singing exercises, opera exercises really. Technique, that thing I used to hate, that I thought was so boring and anti-art, is now really important for the improvisation. It's that thing about absolute control. You are right on pitch, you are standing on one leg, and you are there, and you can hold it and you are balancing. In a way you are trying to achieve the impossible with the technique. You spend all these hours doing fairly mundane, obvious things that are right or wrong, so that then when you go on stage, you can forget about all that, but it's still in your body and in your voice and available to you.

MD: So that is more about learnt, physical technique. What about the technique of making a choice: about an expert kind of decision-making, in the moment? You have a choice whether you drop to the floor, or do a roll, or sing an Argentinean or jazz song.

NC: That is a difficult question. You are talking about that precise moment, the nano-second before you do something. In *Frank*, that is really difficult because sometimes what happens is that there is this absenting of myself from it all, and then it happens without me being there. That doesn't happen all the time. Most of the time, I have an idea and my brain just thinks, 'Ooh, do this now,' so I do it. But that is different than me having an idea before I go on stage, or having an idea during one bit, about the next bit I am going to do. I don't do that. Sometimes what happens is that a second or maybe less than a second before I do something, my brain is engaged, which is my sense of self and it just happens and then I will go with it. I prefer it when something happens and it is not about me, or my brain or my mind – it just happens. That is what I prefer. It's a difficult thing to talk about it because it can go either way. It can come from the mind or it can come from this place of absence and something happens – those are the best moments. I think one of the best improvisations that I did was not with *Frank*. I did this other improvisation called *Fever*, which was with a string quartet, saxophonist and a clarinettist. This was also in Venice and I was really ill, for the first time in my life, I had the flu. It was the second night, which is always weird – doing two nights of this performance and I was out of it and I thought I wasn't going to be able to do it. I went on stage and the whole show happened without me. I remember vaguely a couple of things and afterwards, the producer, Vera, who has seen just about every show said, 'Oh that was amazing, do you remember you did this and you did that?' and I said, 'No, I don't remember' and I just went back to the hotel and collapsed. I think because I was ill and because I thought, 'Oh this has just got to happen'. I was more or less absent from it all, and it did more or less just happen. And I think that is why people take drugs, to get out of their heads and then the thing happens, and I think that is what happened that night. It is really difficult to be unconscious and conscious at the same time. It is this contradiction. You cannot make it happen and you cannot look for it because in looking and trying to return to that or trying to make something happen, you will never find it. You destroy it. It's like trying to make yourself happy or trying to be in love with somebody – you just can't do it.

MD: Or trying not to be in love with somebody. There is an interesting point where you said – 'You are not there, or almost not there', and yet it's a solo...

NC: Yes, there is nobody there and there is nobody watching either, there is no audience. It just is – this is gonna sound really wanky now – it is that moment of oneness, where everything becomes exactly one. And for there to be oneness, there can't be somebody else watching it or doing it. It is moment of absolute oneness. And I think that is why people go to see the theatre or go to see art, because they feel there is something missing, and they have glimpses of this oneness. That is why people go to church, for a tiny glimpse of no separation. And sometimes that can happen in theatre and art.

MD: How long is that moment for you?

NC: Well – there is no moment because there is no time. There is no time at that point. I used to go on about how you have to be present in the moment – you have to be here, now and that is no good for me now because there is no here and there is no now, because if you say there is a now there has got to be a then. I used to have this thing that there is no past and there is no future, there is only the present moment. But of course there is no present moment because there is no time. It's just aliveness.

MD: When I see your work, I see you enjoying what you are doing, at the same time as you are doing it. And that in a way makes me read that you are slightly distanced from it, as well as doing it.

NC: The Billie Holiday song is a case in point for me. I tried to do the same sort of thing with other people. I was in Canada and I tried to choreograph onto a dancer the same kind of thing – it's very mimetic, the body movement – to a Doris Day song: 'Everybody loves a lover'. But it took a long long time – I mean he was a brilliant dancer and his physique was very similar to mine but it took him a long long time to do it, like I do the Billie Holiday thing. He said, 'Ah, I see what you are doing – it is very kitsch and camp but you really are enjoying it, aren't you and you really are loving it?' And it's terribly sharp and right-on, American musical type stuff but also you are making fun of it but you are also taking it seriously and enjoying it. I think that that is a thing that comes naturally to me, to move like that and do that kind of thing. And I didn't realise I did that, until I tried to do it on other people. Before then I tried to put it on the other company I work with in Helsinki. And particularly when you have ten people all doing the same movement, it gets very complicated. It has to be like Bob Fosse and at the same time it has to be relaxed and throw away. So you have this thing inside that is so in control, and absolutely spot on, and your hand has to be there, and like this, and at the same time it should look like it is completely relaxed. You are working like a fucker and at the same time really being just completely relaxed. And finding that is really difficult.

MD: What is the role of your self in your solos?

NC: The role of the self is to get out of the way and let it happen, because most of the time it will just get in the way: the brain and the ego.

We want to be rich and famous, really, secretly. We want to be on television, that is why we are in the studio for eight hours every day. Because we want the love of strangers, we want the applause. You can pretend that it is about the theory of God, or it is about your mother, or it is about cancer, or you feel you want to express something. But all the time, there is, in the back of your head (or for me anyway), really you just want to be famous, coz you can't get a boyfriend or have a proper relationship. You just want the love of all these people. It is about your ego and fame and fortune, or being a great artist, or finding God, or finding yourself, your centre, who you really are, and I have been through all of that and it's just crap – it's just rubbish…

…I also think of myself as an audience, and I think what would you like to see, now, as audience? So I am trying to be the performer and director and audience at the same time. I am trying to please myself as an audience. Of course, I do that with other people as well. But I particularly do that with myself. It is a bit more difficult with yourself. You just say, 'Oh right now I would like you to do this, Nigel'. I detach myself – I go over there, and look, and I think, 'Oh yes, I would like you to do this now, and then this'.

MD: Can you tell me more about your other solo work?

NC: The first actual solo I made was a reaction to being in DV8, and working with people intensely, and making a very dark, depressing, dreadful show. Which it wasn't – it was a great success. But I was having to work really intensely and closely with other people, and all the time I also just wanted to get out and work on my own. I wanted to do something that was a bit stupid and silly and camp and careless and carefree, and be on a small stage, on my own. I wanted to tell stupid jokes, and speak. There was no speaking in the DV8 show, because it was physical theatre.

MD: Which show was that?

NC: *Dead Dreams of Monochrome Men*. So, *Resurrection* was the first solo I made, as a reaction to working intently, and wanting to be on my own.

MD: What year was that?

NC: It must have been 88–89. I think *Resurrection* was pretty awful – I think I sang a couple of times, really dreadfully – because I didn't have a director. It didn't occur to me that some solo artists have a director.

MD: Or a dramaturg.

NC: Yeah. For me solo work is about being solo, it's about being on your own. Because I think if you have a director, it's not a solo, it's a duet, and it's just when you perform it, the other person isn't there. But that other person has been there for four or six weeks before. So you are doing a duet, you are having a conversation with the director and he or she is saying, 'Oh I like it when you…' So immediately there's another opinion. And then if you have a composer, or a set designer, or costume designer, then it turns into a trio, or quintet – it's not a solo. It never occurred to me at all to involve anybody else. If it's a solo, it's solitary, one person.

MD: How did you make *Resurrection*?

NC: I took lots of notes. I had the money months before I went into the studio.

MD: The money came first?

NC: Yes. For me, it is good to have a deadline, a first night. I think it's good to have pressure.

MD: Did you know what it was called before you made the piece?

NC: Yes, I knew it would be called *Resurrection* because it was a resurrection from *Dead Dreams of Monochrome Men*. It felt like me going on stage, being on my own and being stupid was like a resurrection, or a rebirth.

MD: In a way, you have 'titled' the process you were going through.

NC: Yes, the phoenix thing, rising out of what I thought was the death of me in the ashes of *Dead Dreams*. Everyone was depressed; I thought: 'Oh come on guys, cheer up. God, these people really take it seriously don't they? I really need to take myself seriously. DV8, it's really serious; it's so work, it's so art'.

Resurrection (1991) ©Hugo Glendinning

And then I thought: 'oh come on, you are not discovering a cure for cancer or AIDS, you're not saving people in Darfur – you're making a show that white, middle-class people are going to sit and watch. So come on, get real', and I still think that. I still think that a lot of people who are producing theatre think it's so important. To me, when I am doing it, I think it is really important because that is what I do, but on the other hand (Oscar Wilde said it), all art is absolutely useless, even agit prop and political stuff and queer theatre. It doesn't change anything. Maybe one person in the audience will say, 'oh I won't be so nasty to the newsagent tomorrow morning…'

MD: What about direct action? Working with theatre with disadvantaged people, kids, homeless people…

NC: Oh yeah. Well nobody really goes to the theatre. Compared with people who go to the cinema, very few watch theatre. People go to football matches, they get pissed, they have sex. They read The News of the World, they rape women and we kill each other. That is the majority of what people are into, violence and death and sex and pornography. We are a pretty miserable stupid race. It's what we have always done. People don't go to the theatre, or ballet, or opera, or contemporary dance, or political theatre. Of course they do, but in tiny, tiny numbers. My parents for instance – they never went to the theatre, or maybe just the pantomime at Christmas.

MD: So, going back to your first irrelevant solo (they laugh), *Resurrection*. You talked about writing – did you do any other preparation?

NC: Before any solo that I make, there's a lot of sponge work that goes on. I go quiet, months before I go into the studio. I read newspapers and books and watch a lot of television. I go to exhibitions and films. I tend to not go to the theatre, or look at things that are in the same field as what I am about to do. So there is a lot of that – of absorbing. I just open my arms, look around the place and see what comes in.

Usually there is some kind of theme, or a feeling of, 'ooh I think it should be about this or that', because those are my concerns at the moment. It's always personal, always autobiographical, always therapy. I used to think that, actually, and then I realised that, 'oh, you have to go to a therapist as well. Doing solo work is not therapy, it's not the same thing'. Then sometimes, inside my head, I actually see myself on stage doing something, or wearing something. So in *Resurrection*, for the beginning, I knew there had to be a table and chair, and I would start dressed in black, but then I would end up being dressed in white. I knew that months before I did it – months before I went into the studio. And the same thing generally happens, even when I am working with a company. I see, 'oh that's going to happen on stage', and usually it does. It might only be a minute, or a couple of minutes, and somebody will do something to somebody, but I will usually write that down. Yeah, there are those things, and the sponge thing when I am absorbing, and then what comes out in the studio.

Over the years, I have developed trust. I used to think, 'Why am I reading this novel? It's got nothing to do with what the solo is going to be about, I should be researching, or I should be... ' Now I just think, 'Ooh, you liked the look of the cover and you read the review and then usually, somehow, it comes out in the solo'. So I think that is how I prepare, just by absorbing and then by having these little visions, or insights into what is going to happen on stage, and then I just go in the studio and shut the door and it sort of happens.

Actually what I usually do in the studio, is I have a plan the night before, a menu of things, like try this, or try this… Then I will go into the studio and do my warm-up, and after that I will look at my menu for the day and I will think, 'oh, I fancy trying that out'. Certainly, one thing I will do is start to choreograph something on myself to music, or to some text that I have written. So I give myself a definite, obvious task to do. If I did not have things like that to do, I would go into the studio and just feel lost and think, 'Oh, what shall I do? I'll just improvise a bit'. At the end of the day I like to feel that, 'Oh well, all those ideas that I wrote

Hell Bent (1994) ©Hugo Glendinning

about and seemed so good, when I actually stood them on their feet, they were crap. But even with all that failure, at least I have got a minute and half of that song, and it looks good.' There is a feeling of achievement, I've got something.

MD: You've done what is so hard to do solo – edited your own work. So when you speak about seeing the work beforehand, are you talking specifically about *Resurrection*, or generally?

NC: Generally, about solo work. Like in *Hell Bent* I knew that I wanted the stage divided into two and that one side would be the public persona of me, and then the other side, the private persona. It was like my bedsitting room on one side and on the other side was a cabinet and stage and stairs. And I knew I wanted stairs, I knew I wanted the bed. I had made that decision a long time ago – that I wanted it to be about the public and the private. It's an obvious thing, but in there is the whole structure.

MD: Did you approach your other solos in that way – structuring them beforehand? *Resurrection*, *Hell Bent* and then *Original Sin* and *Human Being?*

NC: Yeah – although in fact *Original Sin* was not a solo… It was with a woman, Liz. It still felt like a solo. I had the ideas – particularly in *Original Sin*, I had a script, and I would send Liz drafts for her to look over. Also I had Nicholas Skilbeck, a composer working with me, so I worked on the songs beforehand with him. So I was working with other people. I had to provide lyrics and text and then direct the whole thing as well. The next show, *Hell Bent* was a reaction to that. I thought, 'What's new? I want to be on my own again, I don't want to do another duet, I don't want to direct'.

MD: And what was your devising process for *Hell Bent?*

NC: This was the one where I knew that the stage was divided into two.

MD: You started with that?

NC: Yes, and I was very obsessed with Francis Bacon. It was quite violent and sad. I wrote this stuff about the body being meat, and screaming and stuff like that. It was based on a painting, 'The Desire'. Nicholas was again involved in it – he wrote the music. And actually where we rehearsed was very important. It turned out to have a very instrumental role. We actually made it in a mental asylum, in Lancaster. It was huge, massive and Victorian and was being closed down at the time, so a lot of its rooms were empty. We were in this vast hall where the patients didn't come anymore, because there was only about 100 of them left. But it was great, the atmosphere. You are in a place with huge grounds and peacocks walking about all the time. I would be rehearsing and I would look out the window and there would be somebody in pyjamas, just kind of walking around and talking to themselves. It was fundamental to the show and really influenced it. We were staying in a really, really old building that was like a tower and there was a room with a piano in it, which was perfect for Nicholas. This old grand piano was really ancient – so the sound of the piano was weird as well. The whole thing added to this slightly mad Francis Baconesque weird world that we were in. Always when I make work, when I make solos, they are really influenced by where I am. Like earlier, I made this solo that I toured called *Heroine*, which was influenced by Billie Holliday. I made it in Swindon, and Swindon really kind of affected the work; being in a small town like that, away from home and I stayed in a horrible B&B.

MD: Why did you go to Swindon?

NC: Because Marie McClusky, who is a director, commissioned me to do the solo. And she said, 'Oh well why don't you come here and do something'. And also, I don't like being at home when I am making work. I like to make it somewhere outside. In fact, all of the solos I have made have not been made at home, in London. When I make a solo, I like to completely immerse myself in the whole thing. I want to be completely focused, so there is no distraction. I like it to be somewhere strange, somewhere foreign.

MD: So what specifically would your day consist of?

NC: With *Hell Bent*, I would rehearse all day and Nicholas would be playing piano or keyboards. I was in this vast hall and he was in this side bit. So I would hear him tinkling away, and we would go and have lunch in the mental asylum with all the patients in the canteen, and then we would get together at 4 and say, 'oh how are you getting on', and he would say, 'oh try this'. Usually he would go back to London at the weekends, but I would stay in Lancaster and wander about. There was a life-size mannequin of me in the show. I thought, 'ooh I'll get someone to make it', and then I thought, 'No, I'll make it'. So I spent a lot of time in B & Q, buying wood to make a skeleton and hinges to make the arms. I would be completely immersed. All the time my brain would be thinking about the show the show, the piece the piece.

MD: You were preoccupied by you.

NC: Yes, when we are talking about solo shows, in the end you are in a room for a long time, reflecting on yourself, and it's great. For me anyway, it is really good therapy. Because you're looking at yourself all the time, you're returning to yourself.

MD: Are you? In what way?

NC: Well, it is know thyself, isn't it? Well, for me it is. It is a constant appraisal of who I am and why, a constant questioning of this person. Why am I doing this? There is nobody else to react to, it's just you in this room. Many people just don't do solo work. It seems to be a certain kind of person who does it. I know many people who have tried it. They've made one solo and they say never again. But there are some people who keep on doing it; I seem to be one of those people.

MD: Can you give me a specific example of how you bring yourself into the work?

NC: Yeah, I think so. The very first solo I did, I got into the studio and I thought, 'Oh my God, I only have four weeks and then people are going to come and watch me do this'. And at that point I had this thing about a table. I wanted to stand on the table and sing this song. And I sort of knew that. And then I went into the studio and thought, 'oh well, there is this table and chairs and that's not it'. I came to a complete stand-still. And I had this feeling like, 'I don't want to do this, I don't want to go on stage'. I felt really grumpy and in a bad mood. 'Oh fucking hell what have I done?' It's like buying a television set and thinking, 'oh no, I have wasted a lot of money'. And so *Resurrection* starts with me right at the back of the stage, going on and off stage, and crossing it as far away from the audience as I can get, dressed in black – this grumbling figure at the back, going up and down.

MD: Your feelings inform the work.

NC: Yes, that came from: 'ok this is the way you feel, well, let's start with you not wanting to do this bloody show that you have told them you are going to do, and people are paying for. So let's start with not wanting to do it'. And I think that has informed other solo pieces I did. Now I would make a plan for what I was going to do in the studio, but when you are actually there, at half past ten or eleven, you also need to go with the feeling that you are in a bad mood, go with the feeling that you are worried because your lover hasn't called you and he should have done last night. That is what I meant about a lot of therapy going on, because that is exactly what happens when you go to a therapist. You sit down in front of somebody, and you are not thinking ahead of what you are going to say. I sit down and there is quite a bit of silence and he might ask me a question or not, and then I start to speak. Or he might say something like, 'so how was last week?' Or I start to speak about how I feel – about all these feelings and emotions that are in my head. So it would just come out and the same kind of process happens for me in solo work. I go in a room and there is no one else there and I talk to myself and say, 'How do you feel?' And I use how I feel *now*, and *now*, and put it in the show.

And that is what I did then and do now. Even when I am working with a company I will go in the studio and have a perfect plan. 'Oh I am going to choreograph to this piece of music today when we all start at half past eleven'. [Then] I get to the studio and I am in a fucking awful mood and I just don't want to do it. So I put on a piece of music while I'm warming up – this awful piece of horrible music and I stand up and start to choreograph, me in a bad mood.

To go back to improvisation, when I'm talking to people about improvisation, I often say to them, 'If you're in an improvisation and someone is doing something in the corner and screaming their head off, and you are doing something lovely with a napkin in the corner, and you really are thinking, "Fucking hell, I wish she would shut up because she is screaming", don't carry on. Go over there and tell her to stop, or tell the audience what you are feeling. Use what you are feeling, rather than pretend'. It's not about pretending that I am doing something. It's about using the reality of it.

MD: And working with improvisation is a logical development of this method of making in *Frank*?

NC: Yes, it's what happens in performance, in *Frank*. It's what happened on Saturday night when I was in France. I reacted to the audience, they reacted to me and I reacted to their reaction. All the time there is a [live] conversation going on, between me and the audience.

MD: And the question that arises is, 'Why should they care?' How do you work with that? Do people ask you, 'So what?'

NC: There is a big 'so what', and as you say, they usually expect it to be autobiographical. I did have that thought, and then I thought, 'well I am just going to do it anyway and see how people react'. That question of 'why should they be interested?' wasn't strong enough in me to stop me from doing it. Now, I actively don't give a fuck what they think. I really don't care what the audience think – whether they think it is autobiographical or they think I am lying or telling the truth, or whatever they think. It is absolutely none of my business what the audience is thinking. Again, it is a huge contradiction because of course I care about them. If they all leave and hate me, then I don't like it – it's not very nice. So I do care about them. But really I can't care. As soon as you start caring about what people think, or feel, or how the audience are going to take this, you are fucked. You are fucked, or should go to the West End...do commercials. If you really care, then it is about money and it's about selling something to somebody else. If you really care about what the audience think, then you really shouldn't be doing the things I do – weird art performance things, coz they are not really about the audience. Having said that, I still think that what I do is a show, it's a performance. I do get my legs up. I do show-dancing, I do sing my heart out. It is entertainment and I love entertaining and making people laugh; I am a performer. If I didn't have such a thing in my brain about religion and truth and self and philosophy and all that, I would be in a West End show now. But

Hell Bent (1994) ©Hugo Glendinning

I know I can't do that, because I would be so fucking bored. I am not doing it for the money – it's about something else.

MD: So tell me about making *Human Being*.

NC: *Human Being* was a reaction to *Hell Bent*. *Hell Bent* had three costume changes and all this set and make up. I thought, 'Human Being, just that, Human Being, no set or costume changes.' Well, there was some but it was very basic. There was a chair and a skeleton. I now see that *Frank* was a progression of that. Not only is there no set, there is no real text. So in *Human Being*, I wanted to make it about one person on stage as much as possible, and just about being human. And it was constructed a little like *Frank* is. I found music I wanted to move to and the good thing about *Human Being* was that it was about birth and death – two things that happen in life. I sat down and thought, 'well, what can we guarantee in life? What are we absolutely certain of? We get born and then we die. It's the only thing we can say with certainty'. So I thought – 'ooh well, that is what it will be about.' And also then a few of my friends and people I knew were having babies at the time. A lot of women around me were having babies and I was forty-five. And I wanted to have children as well, and I was talking to my best friend Deborah, and she was saying, 'Well if I don't find a decent man soon, why don't we have children?' So it was about children and babies and birth and death.

MD: Do you always have the idea that it's 'about' something?

NC: For me, it always comes from the words. That is why songs are so brilliant. You have got music going on, which is pretty abstract, and then you have these words coming out. And those work together. And so I, being an actor, really I go for the words. The words are telling you what to do. If it is a good script, you don't need anything else. You just do what the words do. And that is why I like working with songs. I find it quite difficult to work with just music. Also, the starting point is always me. It is always autobiographical. It has just occurred to me that I have never done a piece about something 'out there'. I didn't make a piece about Margaret Thatcher, or AIDS, or being gay. It's always huge great big themes like life and death and love and God, and me in relationship to these things – what I believe in, and what I see other people doing. So solo is about my relationship to the world – quite big, obvious themes, rather than specifics.

MD: So *Human Being* was about Love and Death?

NC: Yes, in fact the whole piece is. The audience never knew this but I do the whole show dead. I have actually died before the show, and then I go on. So this thing, this entity who is doing the show is actually dead; the living dead. I am not a zombie or a vampire, a 'non-dead' thing, but literally dead. And I imagine myself looking like 350 years old, or something.

MD: And the audience never know that? Why not?

NC: I don't think so. Nobody has said. They don't need to know. It's just for the duration of that piece. The idea was that I was a dark, black angel who has come to this theatre to say, 'do this', and in the end I was taken back to heaven or hell, or whatever you want to call it. So that was what *Human Being* was about really, about this dead creature talking about life.

MD: And was it a similar devising process?

NC: Yeah, at the time there was a voice in my head that said, 'ooh for God's sake, get on with it'. I feel like that with a lot of the solo work I have done. Particularly at the beginning of shows, I spend the first fifteen minutes messing about. With *Human Being* I wanted to get on with it, and I didn't. For the first five or ten minutes, it is me approaching from right back stage, dressed in black, singing this weird kind of song and coming towards the audience with lots of smoke and lights. So I was conscious that I was doing this thing again. The introduction would go on for five or ten minutes. That is why when I came to make *Frank*, I decided to go on stage and start immediately – there is no messing about, or not a lot. With *Human Being*, I was not successful in that. I certainly had the feeling that that would be the last solo. And it is really. Why am I saying that? It feels like that, because *Frank* is so different from all the other solo work that I have done. Although, people seeing it probably think, 'well it's Nigel doing his stuff'. Which it is.

MD: Can you tell me a bit more about *Human Being* before we go on?

NC: Well, I toured *Human Being* for quite a long time and that is when I started to do a lot of work in Europe. I was performing in front of people for the first time who didn't really understand English. There is a lot of text in *Human Being*. And then happily discovering that a hell of a lot of people do understand English – because of television, American television and also that if they didn't understand it, it was ok because it was visual. I did a tour of Bulgaria, which was amazing. In this tiny little theatre in the middle of fucking nowhere, and of course they don't speak English, but it was fine – the show went ok.

MD: What did you use in it? Dance, visual images?

NC: Dance, singing, a lot of things happening on stage. It was very visual. I did it in London, at the Arts Theatre near St. Martins Lane, and it was an absolute total fucking disaster. It was like the worst couple of weeks in my life at that point. Nobody came to see it and I was doing it night after night, right in the middle of the West End and it was just awful. Time Out gave it this really good review and Graham Norton came to see it. And he went on the radio, before he was really famous and panned it and was really bitchy and awful about it. So of course the audience figures went right right down. And of course it is not a small theatre – it's sort of biggish and so that was a really depressing time. Yeah, and that was one of the things that put me off for a long time performing in London and Britain. I don't do it anymore because I don't like English audiences. I particularly don't like London audiences.

MD: When was this?

NC: That would be 2004–2005. The thing about performing in England is that the audience always love the show, they love what I do. The worst thing about it is the venues. I am talking small scale now, because I have come to do middle-scale stuff. Small-scale venues in England are the pits, it's just shit. If I was twenty years old, I wouldn't bother so much, but I was forty-something when I was doing this.

There are exceptions. I won't name it, but there was one place I went to – there were three bitches sitting in the foyer bit at reception. They are not expecting you; they do not know who you are, and they have no posters up. The blurb on the programme for *Human Being* was from five years ago, for *Hell Bent*. I walk around the town in the afternoon; there was nothing. Ok, I can handle it, but then, in the middle of the stage, there is a line of bricks which they have just put the dance floor over. They expect me to just avoid this line of bricks. You are changing on a line of beer crates; there are no dressing rooms. I am just too old and too proud; if I was a fucking drag artist, I wouldn't mind. And there were seven and a half people in the audience, and of course there were, because they hadn't put up any fucking publicity. They don't care; it's the English and artists.

The English do not like artists; there is no respect. The English think – this is unless you are really famous – if you are not famous and you are trying to do some kind of performance in theatres in Britain, forget it, because people hate you. They think you are out for a free ride; they think you are having great fun at their expense, because the Arts Council are giving you so much money to do this weird fucking shit. It's all so arty, and we would rather watch the television. And the people in the venues – I mean if you are not Pam Ayres or something – fucking Nigel Charnock, who the fuck is that? He is getting paid to come and do this.

And he is fucking gay and he gets down to his underpants, oh fucking hell! I go to Vienna, I go to Germany – anywhere, except Britain. They meet you at the airport, and there is fruit in the dressing room and they don't know who the fuck you are, but the audiences come and its part of their culture. 'Ooh its theatre, let's go and see what is going on'. The director of the theatre knows their audience, and they know what you are doing, so they get an audience for you.

MD: So you have toured *Frank* in Europe?

NC: Yeah, all over Europe and China and Canada.

MD: Why do you do solo work?

NC: If I was born in another time I would have been a preacher or a priest, rather than a politician. You know I could have gone into politics when I was really young, coz I had a big social conscience, and I could have done that. It is something about standing out there, on my soap box, on my pulpit, and saying these things. Years ago, if people had asked me, 'Is there a message in your show? or are you trying to get something across?' I would say, 'oh no, there is no message, because there are no answers'. It's just mainly making the audience think about things, or giving them a choice, or perspective, or whatever. Now I say, 'absolutely, there is a message'. That is why I am getting up there and still doing it, saying: 'you are like this, and you are like this, and we are like this, and actually it's all a fucking joke, so stop it – stop trying to make your life work'. I just attack, I get so angry. All religions, all faiths, terrible terrible terrible. It's all about separation. So I have this kind of religious zeal…

MD: But that is not all of what you are doing, is it? You are not standing up there and just going… blah blah blah. You do something else – you have music and you dance. Why do you do that?

NC: Because with the audience, there is kind of relaxation and an opening and the best time to try to communicate with people is when they are laughing and relaxed, and when they think they are not learning anything. And then, when they throw their heads back and laugh, then I throw in this grenade. I am constantly swinging, making them laugh and being nice to them and giving them sweets, and then suddenly I will tell them 'you are a load of murdering bastards – are there any Christians in the audience, tonight? Do you realise what you have done? My God'. And then the next thing I am doing is dancing, to accommodate it. So that's how I do it – because I believe in entertainment.

MD: Can you describe to me your favourite moment from somebody else's solo work?

NC: Can it be on film?

MD: Yes.

NC: Seeing Billie Whitelaw doing *Not I*, Samuel Beckett, which is just a mouth. I was just crying, I cried watching this solo.

MD: When did you see it?

NC: It must have been 1990. It was just like an expression of everything I had felt – just the whole thing. It was just a mouth and just words and this torrent of words. I think it is something to do with this person who has not spoken for forty years. And suddenly there is this outpouring, this burst of language, where they can say anything they want. And I love the simplicity and the purity of it. This amazing performance, the words and rhythm of the words, incredible. And it seemed to me a total expression of the human condition in twenty minutes – an absolute expression of the meaning of life. It was just stunning. I thought, 'God, that is everything'. And I have kind of been obsessed with that piece for a long time. I saw it live, once, in Edinburgh – just a mouth, quite high up and there is also a figure in a hood, like a monk, sitting in a chair. I think he stands up and sits down during the monologue – I cried all the way through. I started crying as soon as it started, because I had a memory of seeing the film. It was the first time I had seen it live. You know, it doesn't matter what she is talking about, it's just the whole idea of something being contained for so long and then suddenly, it all coming out. *Not I* – you see it's called, *Not I* – its brilliant isn't it – there is no I, there is nothing. *Not I*. The words, the mouth. She gets a bit of saliva, a bit of spit on her mouth and lip halfway, though, and obviously it's just an accident, it just happened and its brilliant. Then you start to watch the bit of saliva. Because she worked with him [Beckett] – he was there. You think, this is exactly how he wanted it to be said, and she could do it; it's just perfect. Can I also tell you about another moment? When you first asked me about my favourite moment, I thought of a group piece first, then the Whitelaw.

MD: Please do.

NC: Pina Bausch, *Contact Hof.* It completely changed my life. It's the first time I had seen Pina Bausch and at that point, I just realised you can do anything on stage. She gave me this thing: 'You can sing, you can dance, you can laugh, you can talk'. Before that I thought you have got to dance, or you have got to sing, or you have got to do a one-act play. There was one moment in *Contact Hof* where the performer is a Chinese or Japanese woman. There is one of those rides you plug in, a rocking thing and she had it on stage. She came on and she leaned over the front of the stage and said 'Ten p, ten p, I want a ride. Has anybody got ten p?' After a while a man got up and gave her ten pence and she got up and put the ride on and she gets on and it was heaven, because it was exactly what I love. This contact with the audience, the audience are paying you, and then there is this thing on stage, which is from the real world and it is making her do this weird sort of thing, it's like a fucking, a sort of sexual thing, so she is like a prostitute and then it stops and she goes again: 'ten p, ten p' and its like, 'oh yup, you are right, it's the meaning of life, it's the meaning of performing. We go up there, some-body pays us, we do something that makes them laugh and it's a bit fun and sexual and we do it again'. In that one moment I thought – 'Ahh, I want to do that'.

MD: In a way it relates, because it is a solo moment.

NC: Yes, it is a solo moment. I realised you can do anything on stage. I got a message from her: 'Nigel, you can do what the hell you like. There are no rules and no boundaries, apart from the fact that you are on stage, someone is shining a light on you and people are watching you. Apart from that, you can do absolutely anything.' And I thought – 'ok, right Pina, I got it'.

MD: There is that moment in *Frank* where you go into the audience. But you don't just go into the audience, you lie and sweat on them.

NC: I touch them, yeah. It is important for me to make contact – emotional and physical contact, with the audience. Because that is what it is all about; it's about communication, contact, community.

MD: And you do that anyway...

NC: Yeah, but when I make physical contact, people have to touch me. They have to have this fleshy, sweaty form coming at them. And I don't do it until the end of the show, when everybody is relaxed and they know it's coming to the end.

MD: If I say the word 'solo' to you, what are your associations?

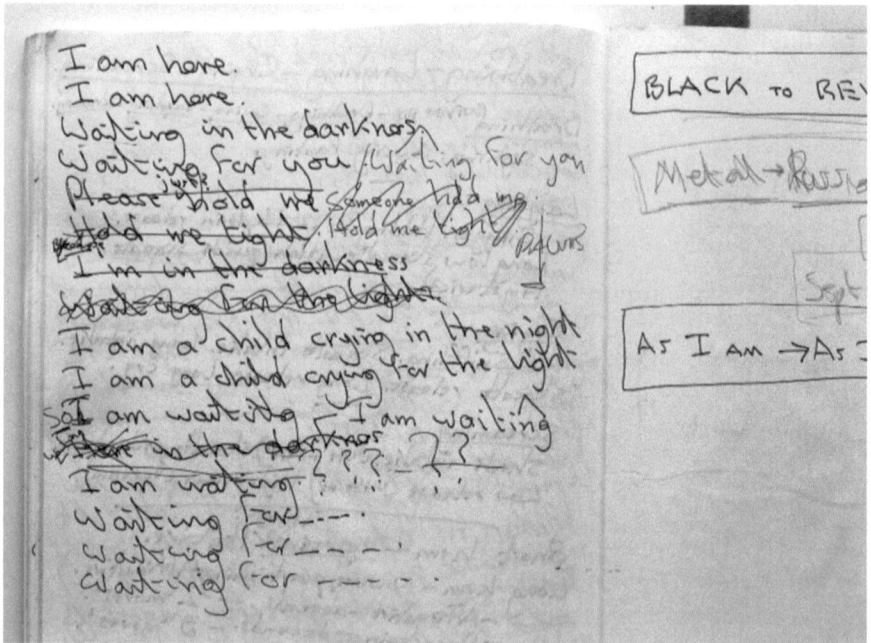

Nigel Charnock Journal entry ©Nick Mercer and Nigel Charnock

NC: Alone. You are alone, you are on your own, it's down to you. You are on your own, not lonely, but alone – singular. You are there. The image that comes to my head is me, of course, on a black box stage – just there, with a spotlight. Like the way *Frank* begins... One person standing alone, in the light, with a lot of darkness around, so you can't see the audience. That is what I see as a solo.

Endnotes

1. This contrasts for example with Pearson and Etchells, who both include significant amounts of written or taped material from others, as well as their own writing, or Houstoun, who regularly invites choreographers like Jonathon Burrows or fellow artists like Tim Etchells to give feedback on her work.

Postscript

Solo – An A–Z of Some Terms

Ambiguity, Audiencing, Autobiography, Apostrophe, Aside, Attention, Authorship, Agency

Body

Creative thinking, Collaboration, Composition, Conceptualisation, Craft, Confession, Co-respondent, Co-deviser, Collage, Communication, Choreography

Devising, Dialogue, Drama, Dramaturg, Director, Discussion

Energetics, Expertise, Eremitage, Economy

Frame, Feedback, Familiars

Giggling, Gaming

Humour

Intuition, Improvisation, 'I', Image, Imagination, Individual, Internal logics

Joke, Juxtaposition

Kitchen

Life Narratives, Labour, Live Art

Making, Monologue, Monologie, Monodrama, Monopolylogue, Mettisage, Musicalisation, Montage

Narrative arc, Nonverbal, New Dance

Orchestration, Outside Eye, Ordering

Practitioner, Practice-led, Postdramatic Theatre, Performance Art, Parataxis, Perspective, Postmodern Dance, Politics

Quantum Theory

Research, Rhythm, Relational

Solo, Solo devising, Solo devising economy, Solitude, Shaping, Space, Soliloquy, Singular, Synaesthesia, Spectator, Self-direction, Sensibility, Simultaneity, Stratigraphy, Site

Time, Tone, Text, Theatre, Theatron

Undoing

Virtuoso, Vision

Wormholes, Weight

Xenocrat

Yearning

Zeami

Index